Living Textures

Living Textures

A CREATIVE GUIDE TO COMBINING COLORS
AND TEXTURES IN THE HOME

  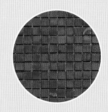

by Katherine Sorrell

CHRONICLE BOOKS
SAN FRANCISCO

Credits

Senior project editor   Nicolette Linton
Senior art editor   Penny Cobb
Designer   Justina Leitão
Cover design   Anne Burdick
Text editors   Morag Lyall, Pat Farrington
Picture Research   Darren Wisdom@Image Select
   International, Laurent Boubounelle
Swatch Photographer   Martin Norris
Illustrator   Jane Smith
Indexer   Pamela Ellis

Art director   Moira Clinch
Publisher   Piers Spence

Manufactured by Regent Publishing Services Ltd,
   Hong Kong
Printed by Winner Printing and Packing Ltd, China

Quarto would like to thank and acknowledge Annette Main
and Frances Eustace for sourcing the swatches for the book.

Quarto would also like to thank and acknowledge the
following for supplying pictures reproduced in this book.

(Key: l left, r right, c center, t top, b bottom)

Asplund: p85t; G.P.& J. Baker: p55; Cassina: p36/Photo:
Andrea Ferrari; The Conran Shop: p19; p24b; p30r; p35r;
p59l; p60; p64; p77; Andreas Von Einsiedel: p102; Fired
Earth: p2; p10; p40t; p44t&b; p48r; p82; p106t&b; Good
Housekeeping Syndication: p73l; Habitat: p35l; p47b; p65r;
p76t; p83; p111r; Harvey Jones: p33t; p69; p101; The
Holding Company/Camron Public Relations Ltd.: p31; p36r;
p42r; p45r; p47t; p49b; p61b; IKEA: p67r; IKEA/Condor
P.R. Ltd.: p72l&r; p76b; p78; p79l; p96t; p100r; p108;
p109l&r; p111c; The Interior Archive: p8- Bob Smith/Artist:
Johny Woodford; p16- Herbert Ypma/Designer: Deamer
Phillips; p17- Henry Wilson/Designer: Colin Duckworth;
p20t- Henry Wilson/Designer: Chris Davies; p21- Henry
Wilson/Designer: Colin Duckworth; p22- D. von
Schaewen/Maison Française; p23r- Ken Hayden/Designer:
Jonathan Reed; p27b- Simon Brown/Designer: Margaret
Howell; p39b- Bob Smith/Owner: Ricardo; p46- Edina van
der Wyck/Designer: Atlanta Bartlett; page 49t- Andrew
Wood; p52- Ken Hayden/Owner: Sue Flegg; p53- Ken
Hayden/Property: Cromwell Tower; p57t- Bob
Smith/Owner: Lassman; p58- Henry Wilson; p68r Simon
Brown/Designer: Margaret Howell; p74b- Simon Brown;
p84- Nadia Mackenzie/Designer: Lisa Guild; p90-Nadia
Mackenzie/Designer: Lisa Guild; p92t- Nadia

Mackenzie/Florist: Paula Pryke, b Henry Wilson/Designer:
Antonio; p100l- Henry Wilson; Inside Stock Image
Production/The Interior Archive: p20b- House &
Leisure/Ryno; p29- House & Leisure/Ryno; p37- House &
Leisure/Ryno; p41- House & Leisure/J. de Villiers; p43-
House & Leisure/Ryno; p62- House & Leisure; p66- House
& Leisure/M. Hoyle; p85b- House & Leisure/J. de Villiers;
p87l- Maison Française/C. Sarramon; p91t- House &
Leisure/P. Baasch; p104; IPC Syndication: p9- Tom
Leighton/Homes & Gardens; p18t- Winifred Heinze/Homes
& Gardens; p23l- Tom Stewart/Homes & Gardens; p24t
Polly Wreford/Homes & Gardens; p25l- Simon
Whitmore/Ideal Home, r Polly Wreford/Homes & Gardens;
p40b- Tim Young/Homes & Gardens; p42l- Mark
Williams/Homes & Gardens; p54- John Mason/ Homes &
Gardens; p56- Polly Wreford/Homes & Gardens; p57b-
Simon Whitmore/ Ideal Home; p63t- Alex Ramsay/Homes &
Gardens; p65l- Peter Aprahamian/Living Etc.; p67l- Winfried
Heinze/ Homes & Gardens; p70- Kim Sayer/Homes &
Gardens; p71- Gary Hammill/Ideal Home; p74t- Caroline
Arber/Homes & Gardens; p91b- Pia Trude/Homes &
Gardens; p93- Tim Young/Living Etc.; p94- Tom
Leighton/Homes & Gardens; p97- Simon Whitmore/Ideal
Home; p98- Kim Sayer/Homes & Gardens; p105b- Nick
Pope/Living Etc; p107- Alex Ramsay/Homes & Gardens;
Kudos Features Ltd./Brian Harrison: p26; p89t ; ligne roset:
p6; p7; p11; p12; p88br; p99t; The Linwood Fabric
Company: p86; Malabar Cotton Company: p88bl; p95r;
Marks & Spencer: p18b; p27t; p39t; p48l; p59r; p63b; p68l;
p73r; p87r; p95l; p96b; p99b; p103; p105t; p111l;Monkwell
Collection:p28t&b; p30l; p61t;Pictures Colour Library:p38;
p45l; p110; Purves & Purves: p79r; p89br;Smallbone: p32;
p33b; p34; p75

All other photographs and illustrations are the copyright of
Quarto Publishing plc. While every effort has been made to
credit contributors, Quarto would like to apologize should
there have been any omissions or errors.

While every care has been taken with the printing of the
color charts, the Publisher cannot guarantee total accuracy
in every case.

As far as the methods and techniques mentioned in this
book are concerned, all statements, information, and advice
given are believed to be accurate. However, neither the
author nor the Publisher can accept any legal liability for
errors or omissions.

First published in the United States in 2000
Chronicle Books.
Copyright © 2000
Quarto Publishing plc.

Library of Congress Cataloging-in-Publication
Data available.

ISBN 0-8118-2950-2

Distributed in Canada by
Raincoast Books
9050 Shaughnessy Street
Vancouver, B.C.
V6P 6E5

Published by
Chronicle Books
85 Second Street
San Francisco
California 94105

A QUARTO BOOK

This book was designed and produced by
Quarto Publishing plc
The Old Brewery
6 Blundell Street
London N7 9BH

10 9 8 7 6 5 4 3 2 1

AUTHOR'S ACKNOWLEDGMENTS

Katherine Sorrell would like to thank her
family, friends, and colleagues for their
constant and unstinting support, advice, and
help. She would also like to thank the
following people and organisations:

The Kitchen Specialists' Association; Andrew
Barr at the Kitchen Clinic; Spencer Swaffer at
Spencer Swaffer Antiques; The Brick
Development Association; Suna Pollard;
World's End Tiles; Totem Design.

Contents

INTRODUCTION

Have you ever walked into a room and felt instantly at home? Or, conversely, inexplicably ill at ease? Such feelings arise from a combination of factors: the room's size and proportions, its light (both natural and artificial), the shapes, styles and layout of the furniture, colors and patterns used and, perhaps more subliminally, the mix of textures.

To consider texture as important an element of interior design as, say, color or the arrangement of furnishings, is a way of thinking that's both ancient and highly contemporary. Human beings have always had a basic need for warmth, privacy, a safe haven to which we can retreat; and to create a home that satisfies those needs is about much more than putting together a few rooms that look good. To be satisfying on all levels – not just aesthetically, but also physically and emotionally – a home needs to feel

right. And in today's fast-paced, stressed-out world, it couldn't be more important that your home is a cocooning, comfortable and relaxing place in which to refresh your spirits and recharge your energies in readiness for the demands of modern life.

Rediscover your sense of touch

So how does texture contribute to all this? On a practical level, using the right material in the right area can be a purely functional choice, from a non-slip bathroom floor to a soft and cozy throw on a bed. On a more spiritual level, however, an enjoyment of all that texture has to offer satisfies our often forgotten sense of touch, our primal need to relate to our surroundings in a direct and basic way. An understanding of this need has become evident in recent decorating trends, which have tended toward purity and clean lines, lack of clutter and an holistic appreciation of our homes (such as the Eastern art of *feng shui*). "Texture is the new color" may be a snappy phrase, but it's best, however, not to think of using texture as following a particular fashion, but to use it as a means of living in a way that's

⬤ This witty, quirky vase is attractive and unusual, and provides stunning textural intrigue.

◀ A combination of smooth, sleek leather with a variety of rough, three-dimensional surfaces demonstrates just how powerful the impact of texture can be.

▼ Mix strong colors and characterful textures for a look that has vigor and verve.

pleasurable and nurturing, thoughtful and sophisticated, practical and intuitive.

To get the best from textures in the home it's a good idea to gain some understanding of the different types of texture and how they work, both individually and together. The basic starting point is usually hard and soft but, just as there's more to color than primaries and secondaries, there are numerous ways of considering texture, with infinite subtle variations and satisfying combinations. Between hard and soft, for example, there's a sort of "giving" hardness, as found in wood, coir or vinyl. As well as matte and glossy, there are dull sheens and satiny finishes; there's rough and smooth, which is closely related to, but not the same as, hairy and silky; there's warm and cool, heavy and light, clear and opaque, dimpled, ridged, creased, frosted, riven, knobbly, sheer: the list is restricted only by your ability to observe what's around you and to stretch your imagination.

Creating a textural room

In general, hard textures provide the backbone of a room and soft textures a gentler counterpoint. Harder textures are often (but not always) quite smooth and shiny, soft ones rougher and more matte. So, without trying very hard, it's easy to achieve a basic textural structure. An interesting, enjoyable mix of textures can result from the use of just two wildly contrasting materials, or from dozens of subtly different ones. A good balance is important, though it's not a question of matching equal amounts of one texture with its opposite – that may, in fact, only result in them detracting from each other. Play around and be open-minded, remembering that texture doesn't just work on its own but has a big influence on all the other essentials of decorating; mixing hard and soft textures prevents a room from having either a tinny echo or sounding too "dead", while three-dimensional textures are needed as a counterpoint to smooth,

◀ Laid-back, neutral schemes often show textures at their best. In this smart dining area the colors used are superbly subtle and the textures full of interest.

flat ones in order to provide visual interest. And very shiny, glossy textures throw light back into a room, while matte ones absorb it.

Think of layering one texture with another, then perhaps adding touches of one or two more. The aim is to achieve contrasts rather than clashes, so it may be best not to pick the more extreme, unusual textures until you feel confident in using them; certainly it's inadvisable to use too many whimsical textures in one space – unless you're aiming for that eccentric look. Don't be too timid, though; rooms composed all of similar textures have no life and will be just as unpleasant to live in as those that are overly stimulating.

What about color, you may wonder? The relationship between color and texture is an interesting one, and the two are often hard to separate. The same color can appear subtly (or even strikingly) different when applied to two different textures, and sometimes it's hard to know which of the two qualities is making more of an impact. Using plain colors, or at least very understated patterns, rather than complex, decorative designs, does, however, undoubtedly enhance textural effect: who needs busy prints when you can have the glorious grain of wood, the linear weave of bouclé sisal, unevenly pitted limestone, fluffy tufts of mohair, or the waffles of an old-fashioned blanket? Keep colors simple and you almost can't go wrong.

When planning your textural themes, consider the room's size and proportions first. Do you want to bring out the coziness of a small bedroom, for example, with a flokati

 A shiny chrome shower head makes a wonderful impression when offset by the matte patina of mosaic tiles.

rug on top of a luxurious carpet, matte-painted walls, velvet drapes and mohair throws? Or would it be nice to emphasize the light and airy nature of a living room with satin-varnished floorboards, glossy woodwork, sheer drapes and shot silk cushions? Think, too, about architectural features. A Georgian house with intricate cornicing and sash windows, for example, may not benefit from over-the-top use of cowhide, galvanized steel or groovy rubber, but needs a more subtle approach, using classic materials such as wood, stone, and glass. In a Modernist flat, on the other hand, where concrete, glass, and steel will probably already dominate, you may wish to use a range of more forgiving textures that will add comfort without detracting from the nature of the building itself.

Structural starting points

When designing a room, one texture is likely to dominate, and it's often that of the floor – usually the largest clear area in the room, and one that can be as understated or as visually striking as you wish. Walls, too, play an enormous part, and while they can be simply painted with matte paint to provide a neutral backdrop for everything else, there is always the option of making them texturally interesting in their own right. These two elements, then, are likely to be your starting point, and it's really worth spending the time and effort (but not necessarily money) on getting them right before you rush into buying furniture and accessories. It's best, for example, to avoid really overpowering textures, instead, choose something that's subtle but still interesting. Points of eye-catching interest can always be created in the form of a rug, wall panel or painting.

Other structural elements – kitchen work surfaces and cupboard doors, for example, or sanitary ware in a bathroom – make a big contribution to a room's textural feel. While practicality is likely to be uppermost in your mind, don't overlook the importance of texture when selecting these fittings. If you have large expanses of laminates in a kitchen you might want to add a wired-glass splashback to offset them, while adding a mosaic shower surround could create the ideal contrast to a plain white bathroom suite.

The chances are, though, that where you'll really get to play around with texture is with your choice of furniture, fabrics, and accessories. Here you can combine and contrast different surfaces to their utmost potential. The possibilities are endless, from a timeless mix of wood, metal, and stone to a groovy choice of rubber, plastic, and pashmina; if you bear in mind all the principles outlined above, you can achieve a look that's not just

▲ In a room that is predominantly hard and smooth, a soft wool rug and woven wicker chair create appealing counterpoints.

good but really superb. Even with nothing other than the careful positioning of a few attractive accessories, you can add wonderful textural highlights to a room that will enhance it immeasurably.

Making light work

The final thought when it comes to planning is lighting – though really it should be your first consideration, as impressive, inventive lighting schemes generally need to be installed before walls are plastered and furniture positioned. Good lighting is not only necessary for a room's function and feel, it will also show off its textures to the fullest. Poor lighting, on the other hand, will flatten texture and make the room seem bland and boring. Try to achieve a compromise between the gloomy dimness of under-lighting and the lamp-shop effect of over-lighting by using a variety of overhead, wall, floor, and table lamps, some of which could have dimmer switches to give you additional flexibility.

There's no shortage of inspiration to help you plan a textural scheme. Buy or borrow

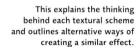 This bedroom balances large expanses of hard and soft textures – the result is both sophisticated and comfortable.

books and magazines, ask for swatches of fabric from shops, keep an eye on fashions in clothing (they'll hit the home a few months later) and generally look closely at what's around, from nature to architecture, people to animals, art galleries to food. Then try to translate what most takes your fancy into your own home. This book will hopefully be an invaluable guide with its photographs, explanations of textural schemes, and swatch files. And the separate Swatch Book can be used to mix and match different textures and help you develop your own ideas.

How to use this book

LIVING TEXTURES IS DIVIDED INTO THREE SECTIONS: NEUTRALS, SOFT COLORS AND STRONG COLORS, EACH OF WHICH CONTAINS CHAPTERS ON ALL THE ESSENTIAL INTERIOR SPACES: LIVING ROOMS, BEDROOMS, KITCHENS, BATHROOMS, HOME OFFICES, AND PLAYROOMS.

MAIN PICTURE

A beautiful large picture demonstrates ideas and themes for you to emulate.

SWATCH FILE

These swatches detail the textural elements used in, and inspired by, the schemes shown on each page. The number of each chart relates to the swatch number in the accompanying Swatch Book.

MAIN TEXT

This explains the thinking behind each textural scheme and outlines alternative ways of creating a similar effect.

DETAILS

Every main picture is backed up by one or more close-up shots which further explain the look.

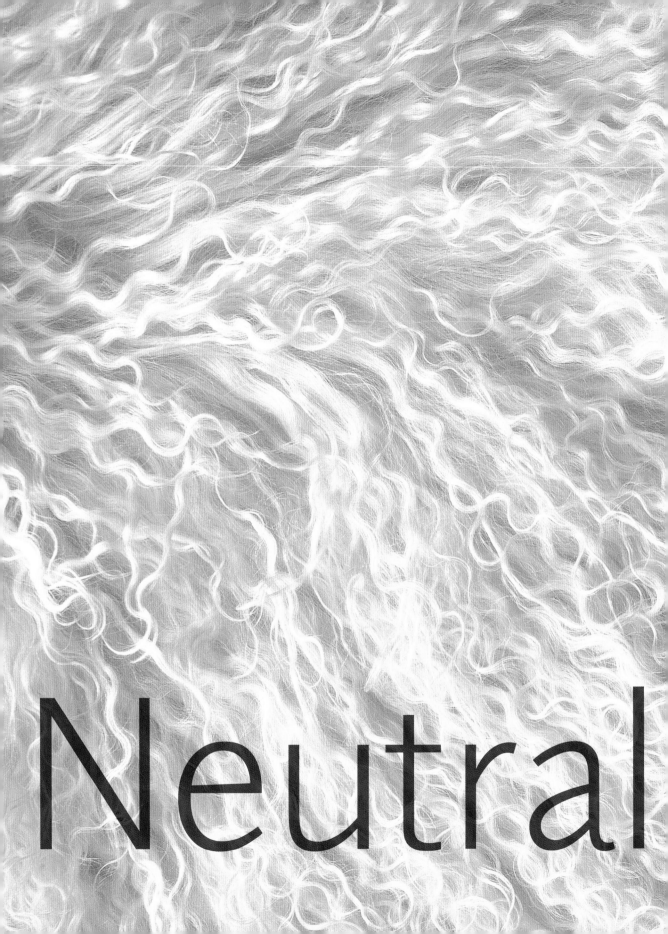

Neutral

THE **PLEASURE** OF TEXTURE IS ENHANCED BY THE SUBTLE QUALITIES OF **NATURAL** MATERIALS COMBINED WITH NEUTRAL COLORS. THIS IS A LOOK THAT **TRULY** WORKS ANYWHERE AND WITH ANY **STYLE**.

colors

NEUTRAL COLORS

Using a palette of neutral colors is the most obvious starting point for a textural scheme, as the less obvious the colors, the greater the impact of the textures. That's not to say that a neutral scheme need be bland or lacking in vitality: there are endless combinations of neutral colors that have a beauty and character all of their own.

The spectrum of neutrals range from black, through gray, to white, as well as cream to chocolate brown via sand, taupe, ivory, and ochre. To my mind, you can also include navy blue and metallics: silver and iron in particular, and, to a lesser extent, copper, bronze, and gold.

Key materials for such a color scheme are, understandably, natural ones. Choose bare wood; fiber floorings; wicker, raffia, and rattan; clear glass; stone, undyed skins, and fur; brick; terracotta, and quarry tiles; and metals. Use with paint colors from the neutral range, and simple fabrics such as unbleached linen, pure white cotton, or tweed in grays and browns.

A neutral, natural scheme may be clean and calm, but that doesn't mean it has to be off-putting or uncomfortable. A pale room based around off-whites could, for example, feature suede-covered furniture, cashmere cushions, a fluffy flokati rug, soft woolen throws, and delicate muslin drapes, while a more masculine room in grays and black might include furniture in leather or burr walnut, sumptuous velvet drapes, oak floorboards and chrome accessories.

Neutral colors are highly versatile and can be easily adapted, not just for any room in the house, but also for any environment: a country cottage, a city apartment, a seaside retreat. Take pleasure in the infinite variety of effects you can achieve: from the sensuous to the dramatic, the rugged to the urbane. If you wish, include a dash of pastel or bold color as a contrast or a concession to fashion, but don't forget that the beauty of a neutral scheme is in its laid-back feel, minimal approach, and subtle sophistication.

◐ In a classic sitting room, neutral colors go hand in hand with an attractive range of natural textures.

◐ This light, open kitchen uses a small range of pale, neutral colors for a contemporary feel.

▶ The restrained colors of this inviting room emphasize its intriguing use of boldly contrasting textures, from floor to windows to furniture.

▶ Lights with strong shapes can be a feature in themselves.

swatch

urban luxury

Choose natural materials for their inherent beauty. Their luxurious textures will help you create a look that's effortlessly chic and simple.

Living room textures

METALLIC PAINT
Metallic paint can be sprayed onto vases, bowls and other accessories for an interesting, inexpensive contrast.
95

TEXTURED SHEER
Sheer fabrics don't need to be plain and boring. This example has a raffia weave for a fabulous three-dimensional texture.
150

SMOOTH LINEN
Plain linen is unobtrusive but has a sophisticated look and feel, whether used for upholstery, cushions or drapes.
179

NATURAL LEATHER
A leather couch like the one shown here has a warm, soft, and luxurious surface. It will wear to an attractive patina as it ages.
226

WOOL CARPET
In an understated color, a tufted carpet or rug can add a delightful bouclé texture that's lovely both to look at and walk on.
259

WOODEN BOARDS
Floorboards can vary greatly in texture. This American white ash is sleek and smooth.
492

Urban luxury

THE SIMPLICITY OF A LIVING ROOM DESIGNED AROUND NEUTRAL COLORS PROVIDES WELCOME RELIEF FROM HECTIC CITY LIFE; WITH CAREFUL PLANNING THIS TYPE OF SCHEME PROVIDES A RETREAT IN WHICH TO RELAX, RE-ENERGIZE AND REFRESH YOUR SPIRITS.

▲ Here, leather and velvet are relaxed rather than imposing and the burnished silver vase echoes the metallic legs of the unusual leather coffee table.

Choose luxurious fabrics and plumply padded upholstery and you won't be able to resist throwing yourself onto the couch and putting your feet up. Pale colors – such as sand, taupe, fawn and ivory – can be mixed with darker accents, or you could opt for a bolder look that makes the most of black, navy or chocolate.

Piles of rugs

A beautiful rug can be the focus of a room just as much as a fireplace or a work of art, with the added benefit of providing softness underfoot. And, while color and pattern are important, texture is crucial: the pile may be short and dense, long and fluffy or, as in the room on the left, cut three-dimensionally for interest and impact. Rugs are enormously versatile (use several different types together in a room for an even more characterful look), and they work

particularly well as a foil to wood or stone flooring, though they're just as nice laid over a plain fitted carpet.

The fabrics you select for a living room are all-important. The gentle sheen of leather can be contrasted with the matte depth of velvet, for example, or coarse wool with the silky tactility of chenille. Window treatments benefit from generosity: full-length linen drapes alongside sheer muslin play on the themes of heavy and light, sheer and opaque, while being highly practical, too. Some modern sheer fabrics have fabulous metallic surfaces, crinkle weaves or even patterns made from opaque appliqués – their textural uses are endless.

To create character, use furniture and accessories that have strong shapes – perhaps round, square, or rectangular – and add dramatic lighting which will further define their forms and surface finishes.

🔺 Mix rough matting, old wood, soft wool blankets, and glazed ceramics for textures with an embracing quality.

Country comfort

NATURAL MATERIALS OFFER A VARIETY OF SURFACES THAT ARE
IRRESISTIBLY TACTILE. IF THEY'RE ROUGH, RUGGED OR UNFINISHED
IN APPEARANCE, IT WILL ONLY INCREASE THEIR RUSTIC CHARM.

◀ Somewhere between minimal and ethnic, traditional and modern, this room has a pleasant atmosphere that's neither too grand nor too eclectic.

It's hard to beat the pleasant informality of piles of fat cushions topping a traditional-style couch. To unify this look, ensure that colors are complementary rather than disparate, and that patterns are muted rather than obvious.

The appeal of craft work

The roughness of a woven fiber flooring and the strong lines of wooden furniture provide an attractive background to the room shown opposite – you need hard surfaces to create a structural background, even in a soft and comfortable living area. And in a room like this, it's ideal to display pieces that have a craft-like ethos, an attractive, unsophisticated quality such as country-style stools, vases, lanterns and wood-framed pictures.

Introducing a touch of bold color or pattern – in the form of a rug, a throw, a painting, or a piece of pottery – can enliven a neutral color scheme without detracting from its subtle sophistication. Earthy or spicy tones are often best, as the geometrically patterned kelim on the left shows. Its woven finish contrasts nicely with the more nubby surface of the coir flooring, which in turn makes a welcome change from walls that have been painted with smooth emulsion.

Think carefully about providing a well-balanced mix of textures – this room, though very simple in style, is full of interesting texture, from the satiny gleam of cast iron and glazed pottery to the roughness of wicker and old wood, to the rather more elegant appearance of a waffle blanket and fake-fur cushion. It just goes to show how deceptive neutral color schemes can be: the effect here is warm and welcoming in an intriguing yet beguiling way.

swatch

country comfort

To create a charming, rural-style room, pick textures that are unsophisticated and unpretentious. Surfaces that are noticeably three-dimensional are important, from thick, soft wool to woven paper, rough plaster to grass-like flooring.

Living room textures

PAPER FLOORING
The straightforward weave of this tough paper flooring is wonderfully textural and would be a pleasure to walk on in bare feet.
297

ROUGH PLASTER
A pitted-plaster wall can make quite an impact – it's a good choice for a living room in which you want to convey a very rustic look.
481

NATURAL FIBER FLOORING
A natural fleck and chunky weave make this abaca flooring superbly tactile. Its informality would work well in a country-style scheme.
295

BOBBLY FABRIC
Cushions or throws that feature bobbles, fringes, or other quirky touches bring dynamism to a country living-room.
121

HEMP WALLPAPER
Instead of conventional wallpaper, woven hemp attached to a paper backing makes a fabulous wallcovering.
309

WOVEN WOOL
Loosely woven wool has the right appearance, providing both visual interest and a sense of understated comfort.
126

◀ Woven baskets come in all shapes and sizes, as well as a vast range of attractive natural colors. They're invaluable as casual storage, and make an easy way to add textural contrast to any room.

Cool character

USING PALE COLORS EMPHASIZES A SENSE OF SPACE AND A CLUTTER-FREE ROOM CAN BE LIKE A VACATION HOME IN ITS FEELING OF FREEDOM AND RELAXATION. THAT SAID, AN INTERESTING COMBINATION OF MATERIALS CAN STILL BE INTRIGUING, EVEN FUN.

Paneling walls with wood is one way to add warmth, character and an inherent beauty to a room; contrasted with them in the living room on the far left is the smooth coldness of a stone slab floor and the ridged surface of the bamboo mat – an unusual item that's slightly playful in feel yet at the same time extremely practical. A fluffy flokati rug or a cord carpet would have very different, yet equally attractive, effects. Smoothness is repeated in the fabric that's been used to cover the modular couch: if pale-colored upholstery appeals to you, ensure the covers can be unzipped and washed by machine.

Fabulous floors

One option if you have wooden boards is to cover them with glossy paint. The ultra-reflective gleam of the floor in the central room shows off to best advantage the timeless yet ever-so-simple combination of wood, cane, and metal.

Good-quality wooden floors, however, are best left bare. Parquet is always impressive, and the example on the near left looks good teamed with a darker wood side table. Classic meets contemporary in the choice of a boxy armchair covered in brushed cotton and topped with velvet cushions, while the hide rug pulls the room together with a defiantly individual attitude. Neutral schemes often benefit from just such a dash of personality, whether it's a striped zebrano-wood side table, a hairy throw or an inflatable plastic fruit bowl. It's a basic rule of decorating: plan carefully, but don't be afraid to be yourself.

△ An all-white room needn't be devoid of interest: matte walls can be contrasted with a shiny floor, while the natural patina of oak and rattan adds another dimension.

△ Animal skins can sometimes come across as rather rustic and unsophisticated; this one, however, is teamed with simple but high-quality materials for a chic, attractive effect.

◁ If this look is simply too neutral for you, don't forget that it would be easy to substitute the rug, pictures or cushions for versions with more dramatic contrasts of texture or color. Or, perhaps, add some free-standing lamps, place a wicker log basket by the fire or stand some ceramics or candles on the coffee table.

cool character

A plain stone floor is the starting point for a mix of exotic woods and unusual fabrics – an effective way to make a subtle statement in a spacious living area.

Living room textures

1 **GLOSSY PAINT**
The ultra-shiny surface of white floor paint reflects the light for a clean, airy look.

WOVEN COTTON
Heavy cotton is hard-wearing and very easy to care for. Give it a pleasant twist with a textured weave like this.

232 **ANIMAL PRINT**
A leopard skin print adds vitality and character – only use it in small doses, though.

BAMBOO BOARDS
Bamboo is a fabulous flooring material: tough, durable, and very good looking.

511 **EBONY VENEER**
Excellent with pale stone, metal, matte paint and natural fabrics.

LIMESTONE SLAB
Though pricey, stone floors last a lifetime and add plenty of character.

swatch

FOR A LIVING ROOM THAT ENVELOPS YOU
WITH A WELCOMING CALM, CHOOSE A COLOR
PALETTE THAT RANGES FROM IVORY TO DARK
CHOCOLATE, AND COMBINE WITH RICH,
SOFT, THREE-DIMENSIONAL TEXTURES.

Warm and cozy

🔺 While the wooden chest and metal-topped table give this room a hard structure, the overriding feeling is of luxurious softness, thanks to the stonewashed rug, the comfortably creased corduroy couch and the knitted cushion covers.

Whether your home is old or new, urban or rural, creating an atmosphere of relaxed indulgence is simply a matter of getting the basics right. A floor in an understated color – perhaps warm sand, dove gray or pale coffee – is both practical and attractive; choose ribbed wool or sisal for textural interest topped with a rug in similarly simple shades.

Walls can be painted with emulsion for an easy, informal look, or else covered with a textured paper: try hessian, cork, metallic foil or raffia for a more unusual effect. At the windows, maximize light by hanging sheer white muslin from a simple wooden or metal pole – its soft gauziness is yet another interesting texture.

A laid-back look

These are your starting points. Next; consider furniture. You will undoubtedly want a squashy couch with washable loose covers made from a comfy fabric such as brushed cotton, velvet or jumbo cord. An armchair might be in leather or rattan (avoid matching suites if you're aiming for a modern yet laid-back look) with a good reading lamp nearby. Suede or leather cubes in different sizes are sophisticated and versatile, while a square coffee table, in wood, glass or metal, adds a welcome note of hard texture to the mix.

Last, top your seating with a variety of interesting throws and cushions; stick to your basic color scheme but use your imagination when it comes to choosing fabric: knitted wool, woven leather, linen trimmed with feathers, fleece, denim or silk, for example. And add a few beautiful accessories such as wooden bowls, leather boxes, glass or gourd vases, paper lamps and, of course, some deliciously scented candles.

◀ Cubes covered in sensual suede or soft leather are a modern alternative to the traditional footstool.

▼ A sheer drape contrasts beautifully with the heavier weight of the knitted throws and tufted cushions on the couch. These, in turn, offset the plain walls, textured floor and rattan side chair.

warm and cozy

From floors to furniture, surround yourself with textures that are soft and giving for a sensual effect that's utterly embracing.

Living room textures

WOVEN LEATHER
An exciting, modern look for cushions, this is an attractive alternative to the usual smooth surface of leather.

225

GOATSKIN
Fluffy and comforting, a natural animal skin is incredibly tactile underfoot, though you may prefer a man-made alternative.

236

CORK VENEER
Instead of wallpaper or paint, line one wall of a living room with a thin layer of warm and visually interesting cork.

306

METALLIC PAPER
Thin, crumpled hand-made paper can also be used to cover walls – or to make inset panels – which have instant textural impact.

314

⬦ Soft, flickering light and delicate scent: a profusion of candles always makes a welcome addition to a room.

▼ Careful consideration has made this room simple but not bland. The surface of the bedside table, for example, reiterates that of the seagrass flooring, while the planked walls echo the shuttered window.

classic elegance

Classic materials are the hallmark of a smart yet comfortable bedroom such as this. Grainy wood, soft wool, and crisp linen all have beautiful understated textures and are timelessly attractive.

Bedroom textures

509 POLISHED WALNUT
Dark and elegant, this wood has a distinctive style that creates subtle impact.

258 WOOL CARPET
The small bobbles of this carpet give it a lively and interesting texture within a neutral color scheme.

186 COOL LINEN
Linen sheets feel fabulous next to the skin – as anyone who's slept in them will tell you.

176 LINEN/COTTON WEAVE
This woven check is sophisticated and simple, with a delightful surface texture.

282 SISAL CARPET
It's hard on the feet at first, but it doesn't take long to adapt to sisal.

241 SOFT BLANKET
Choose a double-thickness wool blanket for extra-special warmth and comfort.

swatch

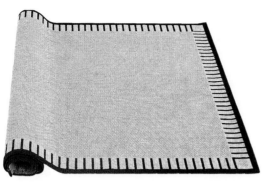

▲ A jute rug such as this is wonderfully soft. The graphic
black edging is a sophisticated touch.

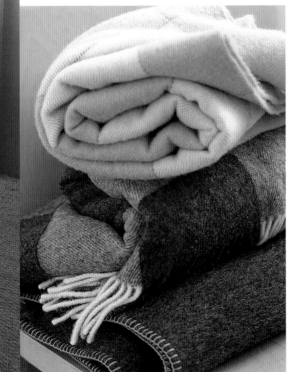

The clean lines of a classically styled bedroom make for the
ultimate in rest and relaxation – no mess, no distractions,
just a beautiful walnut sleigh bed and invitingly crisp cotton
sheets. The trick, of course, is in making it look so easy.

Stylishly understated

A natural fiber floorcovering, for example, comes as a slight
surprise in a bedroom, where cozier carpet is the norm.
But whether you use seagrass, sisal, or jute (the softest
underfoot), its ridged weave gives interesting textural
contrast and provides a wonderful base for a bed made of
polished wood. Of course, if you wished you could always
place a small, soft rug beside the bed. Paneling walls up to
picture-rail height promotes a snug, enclosed feeling; here,
though, matte-painted planks of different widths are a
quirky touch.

Textiles take on huge importance in a bedroom, and
white cotton or linen sheets and pillowcases are the obvious
choice for a pared-down, minimal look. Thoughtful details
such as piping, edging or buttons will make all the difference
between boring and beautiful (add them yourself to plain,
inexpensive bed linen). And layers of warm blankets,
especially in winter, are a necessary luxury. You could
choose white on white with an old-fashioned waffle texture,
or go for the more rustic charm of thick wool that's been
stitched or fringed around the edges – each has a rougher,
three-dimensional feel that's a natural complement to a
scheme such as this.

◀ Generously sized blankets – and lots of them – add a feeling
of warmth, comfort and indulgence.

Classic elegance

DESIGNING A BEDROOM THAT'S COMFORTABLE, ATTRACTIVE
AND FUNCTIONAL IS MOSTLY A MATTER OF GETTING THE
BASICS RIGHT. USE SIMPLE YET HIGH-QUALITY INGREDIENTS
FOR A TRADITIONAL LOOK WITH A MODERN TWIST.

Free and easy

RELAX THE RULES AND LET YOUR
PERSONALITY SHINE THROUGH. BEDROOMS
DON'T HAVE TO BE FORMAL, BUT CAN BE FUN
AND FRIENDLY – EVEN A LITTLE BIT FUNKY.

One of the advantages of decorating with neutral colors is
that they give you the freedom to experiment within a
ready-made structure, so it's easy to create a look that's both
coherent and eye-catching. If you want to avoid convention
without going overboard on eccentricity, think laterally: the
traditional components of a bedroom can often be viewed
from a different angle.

Light and bright

For a refreshingly airy look, you could limewash floorboards,
allowing the grain to show through, and seal them with a
glossy varnish to reflect the light. Paint walls an understated
soft, matte white, but add a huge head board (the one on
the right was made from an old door) covered in a tactile
fabric – think suede, chenille, velvet or jumbo corduroy.
One-color bed linen can be livened up with a witty fake fur
throw, a mohair blanket or cushions made from a variety of
fabrics and strewn across the bed.

Choose bedroom furniture for its appealing character:
perhaps modern and sculptural or '50s style and a little
worn-in. Upholstery could be stretch sports fabric, denim,
brushed cotton or silk. Then consider accessories: you could
contrast a plain, hard floor with a gilt-edged mirror that has
crimped edges, put a basket beside the bed to hold
magazines, or pile chopped logs into a fireplace. And if you
have beautiful shawls, bags or dresses, you may want to
hang them around the room, providing accents of color and
texture as well as a welcome expression of your character.

⬤ A beaten-up chair found in a junk shop sits happily
alongside an oversized mirror – fabrics in neutral colors
but subtly different textures hold this look together.

▶ A large bedroom can be made even more
comfortable by adding floor cushions on which
to read, doze or watch TV.

free and easy

Unusual or three-dimensional textures really help add character to a room. And they will always work well together in a neutral color scheme.

Bedroom textures

TUFTED WOOL
An intriguing fabric such as this would be ideal as an original cushion cover.

122

FLUFFY LAMBSKIN
This Mongolian lambskin has a natural wave and could be used for funky cushions or as a bedside rug.

239

CORD CARPET
This type of carpet is extremely hard-wearing yet very attractive, with a lovely ribbed texture.

274

SYCAMORE FLOORING
Its creamy-gold color and delicate patterning makes this timber a beautiful choice for a bedroom.

504

FAKE SNAKESKIN
This is a fashionable and unusual fabric that would create instant personality even in an otherwise quite plain room.

222

TEXTURED FABRIC
An unusual weave with raffia-like lumps, this fabric could be used for wall panels or as an impressive bed throw.

307

▶ Curving shapes and soft fabrics emphasize the art of relaxation. Combining a suede-effect head board with a fake fur throw could be over the top – but here the down-to-earth nature of simple cotton sheets and bare floorboards tempers the effect.

Soft sensuality

BEDROOMS BENEFIT FROM A FEELING OF CALM AND TRANQUILITY.
WELL-PLANNED STORAGE MAKES A GOOD START, AND THERE'S ONE
OTHER ESSENTIAL – FABRICS THAT IMPLY SINKABLY SOFT COMFORT,
WRAPAROUND LUXURY AND NO-HOLDS-BARRED PAMPERING.

▲ A pile of cushions can have two purposes: for lounging on and as a still-life arrangement that's as good as any piece of sculpture. Here, three very different textures have been placed together to fabulous effect.

▶ The jumbo cord that surrounds this bed is incredibly appealing. Its linear pattern has been echoed in the knitted throw and the rungs of the wooden ladder.

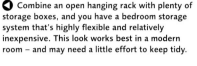 Combine an open hanging rack with plenty of storage boxes, and you have a bedroom storage system that's highly flexible and relatively inexpensive. This look works best in a modern room – and may need a little effort to keep tidy.

The bed frame is frequently the most dominant feature in a bedroom, so it's often helpful to design the whole scheme around it. You might have an antique sleigh bed made of gorgeous grained wood, or a four-poster with slim supports and muslin hangings. Or, perhaps, a minimal futon mattress, a functional painted pine surround, or a no-nonsense divan. If, however, your bed frame is boring or unattractive, consider disguising it with plump padding and a fabric that feels heavenly next to bare skin – such as the soft jumbo cord shown opposite. The softened outlines can be emphasized with layers of throws, blankets, pillows and cushions, made from suede, chunky wool knits, fur, chenille or fleece. The overriding factor must be that they're cozy, warm and comfortable.

Flexible storage

Adequate storage is vital in a bedroom if you're to avoid distracting clutter. Built-in wardrobes and drawers can be tailor-made to your requirements; if you prefer a more eclectic look, however, you might want to mix individual items. A bedside table with several sizable drawers, for example, can hide a lot of necessary but unattractive bits and pieces, and be a good-looking piece in its own right – a curving French antique, maybe, with a roughly distressed paint finish or even some gilding. Or you could opt for an open display of linens or clothing hanging from a wooden ladder or a functional but attractive metal rack – though this may take some discipline to keep looking tidy. Boxes or baskets, in plastic, wicker, canvas, metal or leather, can be chosen to emphasize the room's textural theme or to contrast with it, while changing the handles on drawers and wardrobes (you might like brushed stainless steel, faceted glass or leather straps) may be the finishing touch that transforms a pleasant bedroom into a really stunning one.

swatch

soft sensuality

For a bedroom that's irresistibly welcoming and luxurious, create a textural scheme that consists mostly of warm, pliable, and pampering fabrics, such as suede, silk, wool, and leather. It's old-fashioned comfort given a modern twist.

Bedroom textures

KNITTING Knitted fabrics – whether delicate and sheer, or bold and chunky – make deliciously traditional bed throws and cushion covers.	123	**COWHIDE** A hide rug, cushion, or even beanbag cover would make a funky yet comfortable addition to a contemporary bedroom.	234
SUEDE Natural suede is expensive, but you only need to use a little – perhaps as a cushion panel or footstool upholstery – for it to be very effective.	224	**WOOL CARPET** Though its color is pleasantly neutral, there's plenty of textural interest in the tufted weave of this woolen carpet.	256
VELVET This velvet has a soft pile, a pleasant sheen, and a subtly ribbed surface texture – just right for a bedroom.	200	**MOIRE SILK** This smooth, cool, and slightly crunchy texture creates an elegant, classic effect.	187

The right accessories enhance the textural theme of a country kitchen: huge ceramic jars, antique wooden stools, and copper pans are highly suitable.

Rustic charm

A TIMELESS COMBINATION OF SEASONED TIMBER, BARE BRICK
AND WORN TILES ALWAYS EVOKES A WELCOMING ATMOSPHERE.
THIS LOOK OFFERS OLD-FASHIONED SIMPLICITY, GENUINE
PRACTICALITY AND CLASSIC, HOMELY COMFORT.

◀ **Classic appliances suit a country kitchen perfectly, while chopped logs, hanging pans, and a tiled work surface add textural interest.**

▼ **Though an old dresser might feature rugged, worn timber, a new one can show off equally interesting textures such as acid-etched glass or inlaid woods.**

For a kitchen in truly traditional style, choose a palette of unpretentious materials which have character and attractive authenticity. On the far left, rough brick walls have been combined with a tough quarry-tiled floor in a similar warm earthy color, though with a soft sheen to the pitted surface; the room is held together by a strong framework of roughly cut, scarred wooden beams. The overall result is an appealing unevenness, a rugged, "country" effect that ignores fads and fancies in favor of basic function and charmingly natural good looks.

Inviting textures

Interestingly, there's very little paintwork in this room. Instead, the walls behind the work surfaces have been covered with small, hand-made ceramic tiles, their creamy, dimpled finish softly glazed for a slight shiny effect, while the paneled-pine cupboards have been left bare to show off the grain of the wood. It would be equally effective, in creating a room such as this, to use an old-fashioned wall treatment such as distemper or milk paint: the resulting soft, slightly mottled surface would complement the mix of rustic textures that gives the kitchen its warm, friendly feel.

It's essential to plan storage carefully in a country-style kitchen. Hide modern appliances behind cupboard doors, while retaining open storage – shelving, plate racks, hooks, a mobile butcher's block – to display copper kettles, cast-iron pans, glass storage jars, ceramic dishes, and wicker baskets. For maximum versatility and the beauty of traditional craftsmanship, consider installing a dresser: old or new, it's the perfect addition to this type of scheme.

rustic charm

Unpretentious, straightforward materials such as terracotta, wood, and wool create the right background textures for a country-style kitchen that has instinctive and enduring appeal.

Kitchen textures

578   **TERRACOTTA FLOORING**
Worn terracotta floors, or reclaimed tiles, are found in many period kitchens.

408   **PATTERNED GLASS**
Patterned glass makes an interesting door panel in kitchen units or a dresser.

246   **TEXTURED RUG**
Used on a hard kitchen floor, a textured cotton rug adds softness.

COMBED PAINTWORK
Two layers of paint in different colors, the top layer combed when wet, creates this informal effect.
112

WEATHERED WOOD
When designing a rustic kitchen, old wood is a good choice as it offers just the right textural style.
490

TRELLIS
Fit trellis into door panels instead of glass, or use it to train indoor climbing plants.
523

swatch

Uniquely individual

FOR A KITCHEN THAT'S FULL OF CHARACTER,
AVOID FITTED UNITS IN FAVOR OF INFORMAL,
FREE-STANDING FURNITURE. AS FOR TEXTURES,
CHOOSE NATURAL WOOD, SOFTLY BUFFED METAL,
AND WOVEN WICKER TO PROVIDE SURFACES THAT
ARE FULL OF VITALITY AND INTEREST.

Why settle for a bland, standard kitchen when you could have one that's unusual and beautiful? Long runs of rectangular boxes may be convenient, but they're not necessarily the most attractive choice: often a combination of fitted and unfitted pieces is best, with conventional units making the most of space (and hiding appliances such as dishwashers and washing machines), and more eclectic pieces adding a touch of personality with their different shapes, textures, and colors.

In the pretty kitchen on the left, for example, a hanging pot rack, free-standing work surface and open plate rack are highly practical but also aesthetically pleasing, allowing displays of smooth ceramics, shiny metal implements and wicker baskets. If you have a low ceiling or limited floor space a ceiling rack or butcher's block may not be possible, but removing just one wall unit would create enough room for a storage shelf, rail or rack – even an old flowerpot filled with wooden spoons, or an enamel jug containing fresh flowers, will liven up a dull work surface.

Be creative

Another way to personalize your space is to think laterally. A solid-wood table like the one on the right, for instance, could be topped with a metal panel, and storage could range from oversized boxes made from the palest new wood to containers in antique wood, leather, or even recycled rubber. Wooden or wicker bowls, raffia or bamboo place mats, simple ceramic crockery, and elegant, traditional glassware would all make beautiful accessories, and a modern metal pendant lamp could be just the thing as a lively yet functional finishing touch.

◀ The neutral colors and natural textures of grainy wood, creamy paintwork and unglazed floor tiles are ideal as a background to a delightfully pretty but also practical room.

▶ Layers of texture in neutral colors make for a simple and highly attractive table setting.

uniquely individual

These textures are simple and natural, with a timeless quality that would enable them to fit into either a classic or modern scheme.

Kitchen textures

MATTE PAINT
For a calm, contemplative setting, paint kitchen walls with a pale, soft, matte color such as ivory, white or cream.

2

COTTON TICKING
A classic and inexpensive fabric, cotton ticking is durable, washable and attractive without being at all fussy.

159

BASKETWEAVE
"Country" chairs can be used in all but the most avant-garde of kitchen schemes.

293

OAK BOARDS
Floorboards made from solid oak have a character and integrity all their own. The more worn they are, the nicer they look.

505

POLISHED LIMESTONE
Like oak, a limestone floor will age naturally and has an intriguing patina that provides a wonderful textural base to a room.

527

△ A casual dining table doubles as a food preparation area in this bright and airy kitchen. The different types of wood used have their own textures and characters, but the overall look is relaxed and inviting.

Fashion statement

GIVE A CONTEMPORARY DINING AREA A FUNKY
EDGE BY USING COLORS, SHAPES AND TEXTURES IN
UNUSUAL WAYS – FROM A STATEMENT-MAKING FLOOR
TO THE SMALLEST OF ACCESSORIES, A LITTLE LATERAL
THINKING ALWAYS HAS FABULOUS RESULTS.

Some of the most successful room schemes start with a classic outlook and then develop a modern twist: a wooden dining table, for example, but in deep black wenge wood rather than the expected pine or oak; a storage cabinet, but made of galvanized steel and metal mesh rather than the standard timber; or a set of comfortable chairs, but in flexible, opaque plastic instead of the usual fabric upholstery. Surprise touches can be taken to extremes or kept as a restrained, barely noticeable element: used carefully, they can either update or radically alter a room. You could, for example, simply add felt place mats to a traditional table setting, or go the whole way and cover the floor of a conservatory-style dining room with smooth, round pebbles.

▼ A pebble floor might be hard on the feet but it certainly brings a feel of the outdoors to a conservatory-style dining room.

Shine on

In a bright and airy dining room you can make the most of light by using textures that are glossy and reflective. The floor in this cool, open-plan area consists of limewashed wooden boards, sealed with polyurethane varnish that gives them a soft glow while allowing the grain to show through; the table has a satiny, polished finish and the classic glassware and cutlery add sparkle. The rough place mats are the ideal counterpoint to these shiny surfaces, while the upmarket plastic chairs add another element – smooth yet matte in texture. All this, with just two basic colors, off-white and chocolate-brown, and a pleasing contrast of straight lines and curves: the result is a harmony of elements that's energizing, out of the ordinary and up to the minute.

swatch

fashion statement

A dining room with real ambience and vitality needs several interesting textures – not necessarily funky, but demonstrating an unusual touch and some considered planning. Think carefully about ways to give a classic look an unconventional twist.

Dining room textures

PEBBLES
Real pebbles as a flooring are best kept outside. Indoors, create a dramatic effect with photographic vinyl floor tiles. **350**

FELT
Felt is a versatile material that looks good in modern and traditional settings. Use it for cushion covers, place mats, or throws. **134**

POLISHED WALNUT
Natural wood always makes a good impression. The dramatic grain of this beautiful polished walnut is a case in point. **509**

METAL MESH
Silvery woven metal has an eye-catching texture. Use for door panels, shutters, or underneath a glass-topped table. **458**

▲ This modern version of a traditional doctor's cabinet is an ideal place to store and display glassware.

► The contrasts of color, texture, and shape in this appealing dining room are exciting but not too stark.

Metallic magic

USE METALS IN THE KITCHEN FOR A LOOK THAT CAN BE EITHER FUNKY AND
FUTURISTIC OR ELEGANTLY TIMELESS. PALE COLORS AND SMOOTH, SHINY
SURFACES WILL, HOWEVER, ALWAYS POSSESS CONTEMPORARY APPEAL.

◀ A daring combination of terrazzo, marble, metal and glass makes no concession to tradition. The look is sleek, hi-tech and ultra-modern.

▶ Stainless-steel kitchen equipment always looks good, as well as being practical and long-lasting.

▲ A simple combination of two types of texture can have really attractive results. Here, the mix of wood and metal is well balanced, as is the use of fitted and unfitted pieces, and concealed and open storage.

Versatile and interesting, metal makes a good choice for a kitchen, whether it be as a fully fitted, professional-quality stainless-steel version, or simply employed in the form of a few good-looking accessories. Tough, durable and easy to maintain, it can be combined with other materials for a wide range of effects.

Use with wood, for example, and you temper its inherent hardness to create a warmer and more homely look, whether rustic, chic or, as seen in this kitchen on the left, enduringly classic. Wooden floorboards and a plain, solid timber table are the basis for a gathering of eclectic metal pieces, from work surface to chairs, storage to fridge-freezer, and even the dustbin and toaster. The simplicity of the texture and color combinations prevents the room from seeming too hard or stark, and gives it great appeal.

Space-age catering

Mixing glass, marble and terrazzo with metal will make for an undeniably modern look – or even, as with the unusual, pod-like kitchen on the far left, give a space-age, just-about-to-take-off feel. With a preponderance of hard, smooth, shiny surfaces – especially the terrazzo floor and marble work surface – a kitchen such as this would not suit everyone; but even in neutral metallics, glass and grays, it's impressively bold and dazzling.

If you like the look of metal in a kitchen, but would prefer to introduce greater textural variety, consider rougher, softer and more three-dimensional materials. Take your pick from chairs made of matte plastic, frosted-glass cupboard fronts, displays of matte or glazed crockery, wicker storage baskets or paper lampshades, for example.

---

metallic magic

Hard, hi-tech surfaces go together to make cool, contemporary kitchens. Their impact can be amazing, though if you want to tone it down a little incorporate some

Kitchen textures

337 LINOLEUM FLOORING
It looks like stone, but it's lino – inexpensive, softer underfoot, but less durable.

MAPLE WOOD
The texture of this floor is warm and comfortable – tempering the harsher look

460 METAL MESH
This metal mesh has a fabulous three-dimensional texture - ideal for panels.

METAL TILES
Embossed metal tiles such as these have a sculptural, quite clinical, modern look.

406 TEXTURED GLASS
This texture would complement both hard and soft surfaces.

PLEATED RICE PAPER
Space-age kitchens would benefit from futuristic fabrics for

swatch

hi-tech haven

For a sleek and modern bathroom, look out for the hard, cold, smooth, and reflective textures of metal, glass, and stone.

Bathroom textures

ALUMINUM TREADPLATE
Use metal to cover floors or clad walls, though you should check with your retailer how best to seal it against damp.

474

FLECKED WEAVE
A simple blind at a bathroom window adds necessary softness, offsetting the harder textures elsewhere.

177

TEXTURED GLASS
What could be more appropriate for a bathroom shower panel than bubble-effect glass?

407

PATTERNED METAL
Metal can be treated in many different ways – take a trip to a metal fabricators to get an idea of the range available.

467

MOSAIC TILES
Mosaic can be bright and patterned or, as here, have a more subtle effect. These pearlescent tiles would suit a contemporary bathroom.

435

MARBLE FLOORING
A marble-tiled floor is a luxurious choice. Though an ancient material, it is equally effective in a modern setting.

573

 It can be hard to introduce textural variety to a bathroom, but this combination of wood, glass, metal, and ceramic tiles is a good example of how to do it.

 White paint, white towels and white fittings emphasize the gleaming metal, sleek glass and polished wood in this airy bathroom.

Hi-tech haven

SMOOTH, SHINY SURFACES EPITOMIZE A MODERN BATHROOM. YOU CAN SOFTEN THIS LOOK, HOWEVER, WITH COLORED CANDLES, PRETTY CERAMICS AND, OF COURSE, PILES OF THICK TOWELS.

Hard textures are usually prevalent in a bathroom, and the obvious starting points for a contemporary design are the durable, easy-to-clean surfaces of ceramic, glass, chrome and stainless steel. Ceramic tiles or stone slabs are ideal for floors, though underfloor heating would make your feet cozier; alternatives include wood, perhaps colored and laid in interesting patterns, as in the bathroom on the far left, or vinyl, which comes in convincing wood- or stone-effect. Continue the ceramic theme around the bath or shower, using either standard-sized tiles or smaller mosaic ones. The latter create an interesting yet subtle effect, which could be heightened by the use of a darker grout.

A stainless-steel handbasin with exposed waste pipe gives a chic, industrial feel. You can also buy stainless-steel lavatories, and even baths – though the cumulative effect might be a little too institutional! Other options would be a chrome laundry bin and heated towel rail. Such reflective surfaces make the room seem more spacious and emphasize its role as one of cleansing and refreshing.

In the clear

Glass is a fabulous material to use in a bathroom. A huge shower door made from translucent glass gives a barely there impression, while glass shelves appear to float and, again, maximize a sense of space; frosted, etched or colored glass are alternatives. To continue this look, you could also use stacked-up acrylic storage boxes, neatly holding all those bathroom odds and ends.

Without a little soft texture, however, a hi-tech bathroom might be attractive to look at but would be unpleasant to use. Take the edge off the clinical atmosphere with a few carefully chosen accessories and, of course, piles of towels: in a plain color and neatly folded they'll still appear tidy and practical, but will also add that touch of human comfort that's absolutely vital.

● Though tiny, this room has been very carefully planned to include an interesting mix of materials. The glass shelf across the base of the window is an especially nice touch.

THE WARMTH AND HONESTY OF WOOD CREATE AN ATMOSPHERE THAT'S WELCOMING, COMFORTABLE AND DOWN-TO-EARTH. FOR AN APPEALING ORIENTAL STYLE, STICK TO SIMPLE SHAPES, COOL COLORS AND THE MINIMUM OF ACCESSORIES.

Oriental simplicity

 In an Eastern-style bathroom, as above right, bamboo furniture is especially appropriate. And large, woven-grass baskets provide both useful storage space and fabulous rough, hairy texture.

 As a contrast to the warmth of wood, a minimal towel radiator is cool, smooth and sleek.

A sizable bathroom that's kept clear of clutter has a wonderfully calm and relaxing feel – make the most of the fact that large areas of floor and walls are visible by choosing materials that are texturally interesting. Wooden floorboards, as seen here, are ideal; there is a variety of options, however: they could be new or reclaimed, varnished matte or glossy, laid parallel to the walls or diagonally. You could even paint over them with hard-wearing floor paint. Walls could be covered with matte emulsion for a smooth, sophisticated effect, though a rougher plaster finish might have more impact. For a truly Eastern style, they could be lacquered with high-gloss varnish, though you do need perfect walls to make this treatment look really impressive.

Bathing beauty

Wooden tongue-and-groove, often found as wall paneling in bathrooms, can also be used, as in the room on the right, to clad the sides of the bath. If you want to go the whole way, install a deep Japanese bath made completely of wood: it will undoubtedly be the focal point of the room. To create this overall look, you need to add very little else: perhaps some free-standing storage or a screen; a simple mirror; a rail or shelf on which to place towels; and a few accessories, made of wood, leather, canvas, bamboo, woven grass, or understated chrome. As long as the shapes and textures of the objects are interesting, maintaining a slightly bare aesthetic is ideal.

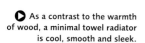
swatch

oriental simplicity

Never underestimate the appeal of utter simplicity. Sometimes luxury comes from thoughtful planning, careful execution, and the use of honest, straightforward materials. Buy the best you can afford, and mix with inexpensive items such as canvas and paper.

Bathroom textures

ROUGH PLASTER
The pleasant texture of a roughly plastered wall provides a good background for smoother fittings in an unpretentious bathroom. **481**

PAPER WEAVE
This loosely woven fabric has a decidedly oriental appearance and would fit well into this type of scheme. **301**

TROPICAL HARDWOOD
Dark and distinctive hardwoods such as this, used sparingly, create a dramatic, Eastern-style effect. **494**

CHECKERBOARD SISAL
The weave of this natural fiber flooring is unusual in that it's flatter than most. It makes a good alternative to wooden flooring. **283**

CANVAS FABRIC
You can't find fabric that's much cheaper or more simple than this. It's tough and hard-wearing, and has a pleasant, flecked texture. **214**

BAMBOO BOARDS
Bamboo floorboards have an unusual grain and a delightful color; they are, of course, perfect for an Eastern-style bathroom. **507**

 The elegance of wood contrasts with the rough surface of the plastered walls in this fabulously bright and spacious room.

A MARBLE BATHROOM COMBINES ELEGANT, UPMARKET LOOKS WITH SUPERB PRACTICALITY AND DURABILITY. IT'S SUBTLE YET INTRIGUING, RESTFUL YET EFFICIENT – A SCHEME THAT COMBINES THE BEST OF OLD AND NEW FOR THE ULTIMATE TIMELESS ATTRACTION.

Traditional values

▲ A Roman-style mosaic pattern made from small, matte marble tiles gives a bathroom a feel that is at once traditional and very up to date.

When designing a marble bathroom, be careful the result isn't too hard and unforgiving – the key is to bring in shapes, colors, and textures that add understated personality. As the stone itself will be dominant, choose a version that suits the size of the room: a very strong pattern may look fabulous in a large room but create too much of an impact in a small one, for example. And don't just think of the pattern but also of the texture, which could be honed to a shiny finish, given an "eggshell" surface or left slightly matte. You can also create interest by setting smaller tiles, of dark marble or slate, into a floor made of large marble slabs, or by laying marble mosaic, as shown to great effect in the bathroom shown on the left.

Perfect partners

Mirror, wood, metal, and ceramic are natural complements to marble. A large mirrored panel, cut to fit a whole wall, is impressive, contemporary and useful; or a smaller, oval mirror, perhaps with a carved and gilded wooden frame, could be hung over a washbasin for a more classic effect. Taps made of metal (ranging from chrome to brass) can be chosen to reiterate your style, whether traditional or trendy, and you may want to add further metal touches such as a soap dish or storage canisters. Ceramic pots, dishes, and hand-made tiles, glazed matte or shiny, give an impression of thoughtful individuality, and the entire look can be completed by adding softer counterpoints, in the form of a fabric shower curtain (lined with plastic), a few towels and a bath mat made of fluffy cotton or woven wicker.

◀ Hand-made ceramic tiles have a pleasantly uneven appearance and offer a subtle appeal.

▼ Smooth, hard and cold, marble and mirror are complemented by the warmer, gentler texture of natural wood in this airy and interesting bathroom.

traditional values

Bathrooms are often based around hard surfaces, but vary their textures and the overall scheme can still be interesting and enjoyable.

Bathroom textures

MARBLE MOSAIC
Small marble tiles create a pleasant surface when laid all in one color, or can be arranged in an infinite variety of decorative patterns.

443

MARBLE SLAB
The graphic patterning of grey-and-white marble always looks smart. Its unique look fits in with all sorts of schemes, whether classic or contemporary.

560

COMPOSITE STONE TILES
Unconventional floorings such as this brick-effect stone would look marvelous in a neutral bathroom.

587

BRASS FINISH PAINT EFFECT
If marble is simply too expensive, create eye-catching walls either with a mould-resistant wallpaper or an unusual paint effect.

120

POLISHED PLASTER
A plaster render like this (properly sealed against damp) has a rough, authentic aesthetic that can tone down smoother, more polished elements in a room.

483

▲ A set of ceramic containers in varying sizes provides organised storage that also features soft color and an intriguing texture.

A BRIGHT, UNCLUTTERED LOOK MAKES A HOME OFFICE A PLACE
WHERE YOU'LL ACTIVELY WANT TO SPEND YOUR TIME. PLAIN AND
SIMPLE COLORS AND TEXTURES HELP CREATE AN ATMOSPHERE
THAT'S CONDUCIVE TO WORK YET STILL ENJOYABLE.

Form and function

◐ Don't overlook the possibilities for textural interest even in such apparently mundane objects as office shelving and storage boxes.

◐ A good office chair is vital. Choose one that's sturdy, comfortable and adjustable: this example is all three, and its soft padding makes a nice contrast to the harder elements used elsewhere in the room.

Whether you use a workroom at home to write letters, sit at a computer, sew drapes, or type up accounts, there's no reason why it should be dull and uninteresting. It must be practical, of course, but it stands to reason that the more pleasant your surroundings, the more productive and efficient you'll be at your work.

Home offices in neutral colors tend to be calm and contemplative, and using plenty of white or very pale colors emphasizes natural light. The all-white office shown on the far left, for example, contains plenty of efficient storage, and a lack of clutter helps to increase its bright, spacious feel. Without the distraction of mess or lots of clashing colors it would be easy to get down to work in here – even the various textural elements used in the room have been carefully co-ordinated to minimize visual disturbance. From the soft matte walls to the satiny floor, the sheer blind to the limed-wood tabletop, they gently complement each other without fuss or confusion.

Adding to the atmosphere

The accessories you choose can make a huge difference to the look and feel of a workroom. In the main picture, for example, a mirror-faced clock, brushed-metal lampshade, and ridged tin-can pen holders add elements of textural contrast; their informal appearance suits this room well. You could include storage in the form of tall metal shelves, as seen on the left, or take a businesslike approach with the addition of, say, a sleek, modern desk lamp and co-ordinating necessities such as box files, pen trays, pencil sharpeners, staplers, and hole punchers. Of course, if you were tired of neutrals, this is your chance to add bold impact and a splash of color in the form of office essentials in bright, cheerful and invigorating shades.

swatch

form and function

Avoid distractions in a home office by choosing textures that are quiet and simple, yet attractive and appealing. Try a mixture of matte emulsion, leather, wool, felt, paper, and sophisticated linen.

Home office textures

WHITE PAINT
Nothing could be simpler and more straightforward than using plain white paint on walls for a subtle background.
1

GALWAY LINEN
This linen has a subtle weave that makes it a comfortable addition to an understated office.
183

NATURAL LEATHER
A good chair can be the focus of a home office, especially when the surroundings are plain. Cover it in leather for sophisticated impact.
226

FINE WOOL CARPET
This carpet is soft underfoot without being too luxurious. Its ribbed texture makes a change from loops or cut pile.
270

THICK FELT
Soft and warm, felt adds an unexpected but extremely welcome texture to a home working environment.
137

TEXTURED WALLPAPER
If you feel your walls need slightly more than plain white paint, consider textured wallpaper.
312

▲ A directional desk lamp is both useful and beautiful.

Back to basics

▼ A classic table lamp such as this is ideal with a traditional-style desk.

▶ The agreeable hairy roughness of coir matting creates a friendly feel here – it's inexpensive and durable, too.

GET AWAY FROM THE STRESSES OF A MODERN WORKING LIFE WITH A HOME OFFICE THAT HAS EVERY TRADITIONAL COMFORT. YOU CAN CREATE A RELAXING ATMOSPHERE YET STILL ENJOY THE BENEFITS OF MODERN TECHNOLOGY.

The basics for a functional home office are a spacious desk that's at the right height for you, a comfortable chair, adequate storage and good lighting; though if you don't spend hours in the office then you needn't worry about the chair being infinitely adjustable, and a traditional-style lamp may be just as good as a flexible, hinged-arm type. Consider what works best for you, remembering that you can always hide a modern fax or answering machine inside an antique cabinet, and that it's easily possible to make an office really homely by incorporating a fireplace, pictures on the walls, old-fashioned telephone and plenty of ornaments. A squashy couch piled up with soft cushions and throws may be just the place for quiet contemplation, and an assortment of books will look especially nice on open shelving.

Gentle contrasts

Making good use of texture will really bring this sort of room to life: your aim is to create a cozy, welcoming feel by using robust, natural materials. Avoid the overly modern look of plastic, rubber or stainless steel; instead think of contrasting rough and smooth, hard and soft in a gentle, unimposing way by using coir flooring, tactile rugs – perhaps made of natural hide or wool with a deep, giving pile – old wood (for paneling walls or as a desk with brass-handled drawers) and accessories in leather, paper, suede or matte metal.

A silk shade combined with a ceramic lamp base is one good choice for lighting, while another would be a brass base with a frosted glass shade; as with other furnishings in this type of scheme, they both offer a satisfying combination of textures together with absolute practicality and a suitably familiar, classic design.

▲ String has been glued in patterns to the surface of this timber desk, and makes an intriguing and exciting texture.

◀ Storage boxes made of leather have an air of quiet sophistication.

back to basics

Surround yourself with traditional comforts and make a work space that's welcoming and enjoyable to be in. Combine classic wood and leather with the more contemporary looks of sisal and cowhide.

Home office textures

234 **COWHIDE**
Funky but functional, this rug will update any room and makes for a dynamic office.

227 **PIERCED LEATHER**
Leather – even when pierced – is upmarket, comfortable, and timeless.

167 **TEXTURED COTTON**
A classic woven cotton complements a range of other textures.

282 **SISAL CARPET**
Sisal flooring is ideal for a home office – durable, easy to clean, and good-looking in an understated way.

127 **SOFT LAMBSWOOL**
The soft and fluffy, bouclé texture of this woolen fabric is unexpected, yet ideal for an office.

493 **EXOTIC WOOD**
Tropical hardwood gives the impression of high quality and enduring luxury.

swatch

Soft

SOFT COLORS ARE **EASY** TO PUT TOGETHER, AND ALWAYS **CREATE** HARMONIOUS, WELCOMING AND RELAXING SCHEMES. USE THEM TO HIGHLIGHT **GENTLE** CONTRASTS AND COMBINATIONS OF TEXTURES TO **DELIGHTFUL** EFFECT.

colors

SOFT COLORS

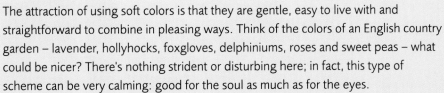

A combination of several muted colors is calm and pretty in this light-filled dining area.

Using peach-colored paintwork with an aluminum floor might be unexpected, but it's certainly effective.

The attraction of using soft colors is that they are gentle, easy to live with and straightforward to combine in pleasing ways. Think of the colors of an English country garden – lavender, hollyhocks, foxgloves, delphiniums, roses and sweet peas – what could be nicer? There's nothing strident or disturbing here; in fact, this type of scheme can be very calming: good for the soul as much as for the eyes.

Soft colors include knocked-back versions of primaries in the form of pink, baby blue, and lemon yellow, and pale secondary shades such as lilac, mint green, and peach. Of course, there may only be a subtle difference between a pink that is soft and a pink that is strong; the key is to choose shades that won't dazzle or demand too much, but that simply contribute to the room's overall harmony. And, while a scheme could be based completely around one soft color, two together, or indeed several, there's nothing wrong with adding a bolder shade for extra emphasis (think of the impression you could make by combining fuchsia with lilac and pale pink, for example, or turquoise with watery blue and lemon) or using neutral colors as a background. Metal surfaces, especially brushed stainless steel, and pale, grained woods look particularly good when combined with soft colorways. That's the great thing about soft shades: you can do almost anything you like with them and they still look fabulous.

Natural materials can make a good starting point for a soft color scheme: it's surprising how many of them come in gentle but colorful shades. Slate, for example, usually thought of as gray, can also be tinged a delicate pink, purple or green, while marble and terrazzo offer a wealth of lovely colors. Plaster, too, either in its natural pink or in tinted form, has a soft tone that's highly attractive. Colored glassware and ceramic tiles, crockery or vases make a wonderful basis for decorating in soft colors, while textiles, carpets and rugs can contribute enormously to a delightful scheme such as this.

A fake fur throw provides a luscious counterpoint on a traditional couch. Here, roughly textured wood and industrial metal add an informal feel.

Timeless good taste

THE GENTLE CALMNESS OF SOFT COLORS CAN GIVE A LIVING ROOM ENORMOUS APPEAL. MAKE THE MOST OF TACTILE MATERIALS BY CREATING A LOOK THAT'S LUXURIOUS YET UNCLUTTERED, WITH POISE, CLASS AND QUIET SOPHISTICATION.

One way to approach the design of a living room is to base it around a beautiful fabric in a cool, muted shade. The fabric could be used for drapes or furniture, a throw or even a wall-hanging. You can then choose other colors, textures and materials that bring out its best qualities. These two traditional couches, for example, have been covered in a linen/cotton fabric that is hard-wearing and highly attractive, smooth yet with a noticeable crisp weave.

Layer upon layer

Having chosen a main fabric, the next step is to build up the different textures around it, bearing in mind that this look requires a minimum of decorative flourishes and absolutely no fussy details. It may be best to keep walls pale and quite smooth in order to provide a quiet background against which everything else will stand out. On the floor, rough boards washed with thinned-down white paint give a casual, off-the-cuff flourish, while smooth, shiny parquet has a more upmarket air. Or you could try a wool carpet, sisal flooring, or even rubber or metal floor tiles.

Finally, add tufted, woven or shagpile rugs, and one or two pieces of furniture, perhaps made from worn, reclaimed wood or gleaming glass. Don't forget lamps: in traditional ceramic, glass with paper or silk, or workmanlike metal. Throws and cushions could be in the same fabric as the couch with unusual buttons or a pretty trimming, or in a different fabric entirely, providing a glamorous contrast.

 The textures in this room have been subtly contrasted. Apart from the slightly rough weave of the couch fabric, everything is smooth and shiny in varying degrees.

timeless good taste

Natural materials such as wood, hide, and muslin are the basics for a living room scheme that is calm and quiet. Their textures are beautifully complementary and have an unfussy, classic appearance.

Living room textures

515 RED OAK FLOORING
Timber floors look good, last well, and wear beautifully – a perennial favorite.

236 GOATSKIN
Soft and shaggy, a furry throw or rug (real or fake) adds a cozy touch.

281 RIBBED SISAL
This rough, hairy flooring brings softer textures into focus.

142 SHEER MUSLIN
A delicate cotton muslin – here in an unusual apple green – is a good choice for a softly gathered drape.

206 SOFT CHENILLE
An appealing fabric for upholstery or drapes, chenille is irresistibly tactile.

334 MARBLED PAPER
This wallpaper is a subtle and upmarket option for a traditional living room.

swatch

Forces of nature

BE INSPIRED BY NATURAL SHADES AND CREATE
A FRESH LOOK FOR A LIVING ROOM. NEITHER
TRADITIONAL NOR TRENDY, GENTLE COLORS AND
TEXTURES WORK TOGETHER EFFORTLESSLY AND
HAVE A TIMELESS, ENDURING APPEAL.

A living room designed around a natural theme is very pretty – as can be seen in the relaxed, comfortable room shown in the main picture. When putting together such a scheme, find colors that complement each other in an interesting, but not too dramatic, way. It may help to think of the seasons: warm russets and browns for the fall, deeper reds and aubergines for winter, fresh limey yellows and greens for spring, and pretty lavender, sky blue, and pink for summer.

Transformation time

You'll find that textures for this scheme follow on quite readily. Again, take as your starting point the natural world and note the wonderful variety that you could introduce: perhaps woven willow, tree bark, birds' eggs, soft fur, rounded pebbles or worn stone, to name but a few. In this scheme, the basic textures are the ribbed carpet and a wall painted a pale pastel-green. The main item of furniture, a two-seat couch, has been completely covered by a chenille throw. As well as introducing another textural element, this is an ideal way to disguise a chair or couch that's badly worn or doesn't fit into your color scheme – but do ensure that your throw is large enough to cover the piece entirely, and tuck it well into the sides and back so it doesn't ruck up as soon as someone sits on it.

The finishing touches are some more cozy throws, cushions with textures that range from suede to smocking, and some carefully chosen accessories including a basketweave bag, crackleglaze vase, and paper lamp shade. As can be seen in the pictures top right and bottom left, thoughtful details such as a cushion made from an innovative fabric or a careful grouping of pretty ceramics can be incredibly effective. Without a doubt, this is a look that's inexpensive and easy to emulate.

swatch

forces of nature

From crunchy leaves and woven leather to grained wood and softly ribbed wool, the textures of nature can be combined and contrasted to create a delicious scheme for a living room.

Living room textures

FALL LEAVES
More or less any surface can be photographed and transferred onto vinyl floor tiles. These leaves look particularly effective.

351

SISAL CARPET
Natural fiber floorings are made in various weaves; this medium-ribbed version could be used almost anywhere in the house.
285

WOVEN LEATHER
Natural but still sophisticated, woven leather makes an ideal covering for a cushion in a scheme of this type.

225

MAPLE VENEER
Veneer panels, though not inexpensive, make a superb covering for a wall – or maybe just a small section of a wall.

512

MATTE PAINT
Choose a soft, fresh color of matte paint, distemper or milk paint with which to cover one or more walls.
49

RIBBED WOOL
This woolen fabric echoes the sisal carpet, but makes a nice complement as it's soft and giving rather than rough and hairy.
131

▶ Matte on matte – the muted color and texture of these bottle-shaped vases, set against a painted fire surround, make a delightful and subtle combination.

▶ Against the background of a smooth, matte-painted wall, there is a range of warm, soft textures in this room. The small wooden cupboard with ribbed rattan doors makes an excellent, quiet counterpoint.

This cushion fabric has a fabulous, unusual texture – it's emphasized by the smooth background of the chair fabric and a wall covered in large panels of beautiful, unpainted wood.

⬤ An eclectic choice of textures works well in this fashion-conscious room.

Fresh vision

WHETHER YOU CHOOSE TRADITIONAL, CONTEMPORARY OR
UNUSUAL MATERIALS, A COMBINATION OF WARM, SOFT SHADES
WILL HELP CREATE A LIVING ROOM THAT'S FRIENDLY AND INVITING.

The color family that stretches from red through pink to lilac and plum has instant human appeal, but the effects of individual shades can be very different. Rose pink and pale mauve, for example, are pretty and delicate; bubble gum and scarlet lively and invigorating; and the darker aubergine shades luxurious and cozy. Add to this the impact of form and texture and the results can be stunning.

Fashionable – and fun

In the modern room above, a designer chair upholstered in bold stretch fabric is the basis for a look that's eclectic and funky. The chair itself contrasts the matte softness of the textile with smooth, shiny metal, while the painted plaster walls feature a metal-trimmed display shelf; large vases in glass and acrylic add yet another texture to the mix. The

overall result is bold and exciting, yet still easy to live with. Other materials that would work in this type of room might include rubber, plastic, vinyl, concrete, flokati and, if you like a no-holds-barred look, maybe even some whimsical ones such as bubble wrap and Astroturf.

For an even softer look, choose a classic designer chair upholstered in dark, intense leather, like the one in the modern living room on the right, which has a warmth and tactile quality that forces you to relax. The sumptuous nature of this comfortable corner is further emphasized by the deep-pile woolen rug and curving shapes of the chair and footstool, the wooden side table, and acrylic magazine rack. It's a subtle, upmarket, and informal combination of color, shape, and texture that creates an immediate, yet understated, impact.

fresh vision

By cleverly contrasting different textures, you can create rooms that are interesting both to look at and to live in.

Living room textures

FAKE LEATHER
Exciting and original in texture and color, this fabric would be great for upholstery, cushions or a beanbag cover.

220

SHEEPSKIN
Soft, fluffy, and shaggy, sheepskin is attractive and easygoing, and looks good on wooden or natural fiber floors.

237

LINOLEUM FLOORING
Lino would probably not be most people's first choice for a living area, but with an interesting texture it can be highly effective.

343

TEXTURED GLASS
The opacity of glass means it's a good way to add texture without cluttering a room – ideal for shelving, bowls, vases or drinking glasses.

404

▼ This side table contrasts dark oak with clear glass set against smooth walls painted in warm, soft colors. The silver lining of the wooden bowl gives a modern twist to a classic accessory.

▲ Wood, acrylic, and shiny metal make a good contrast to the softness of leather and wool.

▲ Accessories such as ceramic bowls, wooden picture frames and, of course, fresh flowers really help to complete a sensual bedroom scheme.

A calm retreat

SOFT COLORS REALLY COME INTO THEIR OWN IN THE BEDROOM, WHERE THEY HELP TO SOOTHE AWAY THE STRESSES OF THE DAY. COMBINE WITH A VARIETY OF INTERESTING, LUXURIOUS TEXTURES TO CREATE AN INDULGENT HAVEN.

When you use generous amounts of fabric in a bedroom it results in a floaty, feminine look, particularly when colors are restricted to the paler end of the palette. Sheer muslin, or a gathered length of unbleached linen, looks fabulous at a window (and lets in plenty of light), and it's easy to make drapes for a four-poster bed by sewing simple ties along one edge of a standard sheet or ready-made drape.

The plainest bed linen can be enlivened with subtle piping,

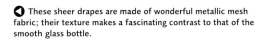

◀ These sheer drapes are made of wonderful metallic mesh fabric; their texture makes a fascinating contrast to that of the smooth glass bottle.

swatch

a calm retreat

Choose giving, informal textures with which to build up layers of luxury and create a bedroom that's sensuous, calming and relaxing.

Bedroom textures

BRUSHED PAINT EFFECT
A gentle paint effect can give a warmer impression than plain-painted walls, without being overbearing or intrusive.
107

THICK FELT
Though an inexpensive and utilitarian fabric, the thick, soft texture of felt creates an impression of attainable opulence.
135

SHEER DRAPES
Sheer fabric is pretty even when plain, but a small, sweet pattern can add decorative impact at the window.
147

WOOL BLANKET
Like felt, wool has eternal, old-fashioned appeal. Its warmth and comfort are always a benefit in a cozy bedroom.
243

BASKETWEAVE
Woven cane – for chair seats, blinds, or wall coverings – has a charm and faintly rustic air that works in a peaceful room.
292

ELM WOOD
Classic bedroom furniture – made of beautiful, natural wood – is always a good partner to elegant and indulgent fabrics.
498

buttons, ties or borders, and you can add a touch of luxury with a casual throw or by adding piles of cushions made from soft, felted or knitted wool, velvet, cashmere, pashmina, or silk satin.

Tactile patinas

If you're aiming for an informal, country look, a good complement to all this fabric would be to choose furniture and accessories made from harder, rougher wood and wicker. Wooden pieces, whether chests, beds, chairs, trays, or bowls, could be precisely made, Shaker-style in maple or cherry, highly polished antique pieces, or beaten-up second-hand versions with a characterful patina; wicker baskets of all shapes and sizes come in a range of lovely, gentle colors and interesting weaves, while rounded wicker chairs always seem to fit well into this type of scheme.

On the floor, a soft carpet is kind to bare feet, or you could place a rug on top of either wooden boards – painted, stained, varnished or oiled – or a natural fiber floorcovering made from jute, sisal or seagrass. Walls could perhaps be bare brick, rough plaster or painted wooden paneling, while lighting is best kept low and romantic (though do remember to provide good directional light for mirrors and dressing areas), with lamps in a variety of shapes and sizes made from wood, ceramic, glass, paper, silk, and raffia.

◀ Lidded wicker baskets are a good-looking method of storage. An alternative might be a large wooden chest which could, with a cushion on top, double as a seat.

Relaxed grandeur

USE ANTIQUE PIECES TO GIVE A BEDROOM A
SENSE OF OCCASION – COMBINED WITH MUTED
COLORS AND TACTILE FABRICS THEY NEEDN'T
BE OVER-IMPOSING. YOU CAN COMBINE
COMFORT WITH A SURE SENSE OF STYLE.

The textures in a bedroom tend to be soft and smooth, warm and giving, which is ideal for creating an atmosphere of sensual relaxation. For variety and interest, however, it's good to include touches of harder or rougher textures.

In the striking green bedroom to the right, for example, a white carpet with a dense, low pile provides a forgiving base, while the chaise-longue and bed are upholstered in luxurious velvet and padded cotton respectively. Pretty bed linen and a sheer muslin drape over the headboard contribute to the overall effect of luxurious tranquility.

Structured sensuality

The bed's carved wooden frame, however, together with the antique wardrobe and, especially, the metal corona above the head board, add a hard structure to the room that gives the design an interesting edge. The large mirror on the wardrobe is another pleasantly hard, smooth surface, with the added benefit of being placed opposite the window so as to reflect light into the room. Meanwhile, the metal lamp base echoes the form and material of the chandelier, but is downplayed by its plain paper shade.

Bed linen itself can also provide a variety of textures. Though sheets, pillowcases and duvet covers are usually made from plain cotton, polycotton or linen, they could have interesting edging, buttonholes or borders, and blankets, throws and cushions might be made from knitted chenille, thick soft wool, warm felt, fake fur, smooth silk or old-fashioned waffle.

swatch

relaxed grandeur

Rooms containing textures that are all too similar will inevitably be bland and boring. Mix hard and soft, rough and smooth materials with careful consideration to create a bedroom that has a sumptuous, sophisticated look and a relaxing, inviting feel.

Bedroom textures

WOVEN JACQUARD
Intricate and subtle, the textures of a self-colored weave brings a tailored classicism to a bedroom scheme.

170

TEXTURED WALLPAPER
This smart wallpaper isn't overly eye-catching, but makes a pleasant textural change from smooth paintwork.
320

LIMED WOOD
Liming wood emphasizes its grain and allows you to tone it gently with colors used elsewhere.

116

ROUGH PLASTER
Tinted and pitted plaster is another wall treatment that's unusual without being overbearing.
487

QUILTED VELVET
A strong diamond pattern distinguishes this fabric – it would be fantastic as a luxurious bed throw.

211

RUSH FLOORING
Softer underfoot than both sisal and coir, rush is a delightful flooring with an interesting woven texture.
280

▶ The ribbed texture of these throws and blankets would look great against a plain, smooth duvet cover.

△ Used with plain walls and carpet as well as pretty textiles, the antique pieces in this room are attractive and comfortable without being awe-inspiring.

◁ Chambray bed linen made from a mix of cotton and polyester is both soft against the skin and easy to wash.

Light and inviting

A BEDROOM CAN BE WARM AND WELCOMING
WHILE STILL LOOKING FASHIONABLY MODERN. THE
KEY IS TO AVOID CLUTTER, USE PLAIN AND SIMPLE
FURNISHINGS AND CHOOSE PRETTY COLORS
COMBINED WITH IRRESISTIBLE TEXTURES.

Sometimes just one gorgeous texture can have a big impact on a room, and in a bedroom the thing that usually stands out most is the bedcover. Choose one in a fairly subtle color and it will emphasize a warm and cozy texture all the more – whether it be made of fleece, mohair, velvet, wool or silk. Match it with a few scatter cushions against smooth cotton or linen pillows and you'll create a beautiful basis around which to design the room.

Keep it simple

For this type of look the Mies van der Rohe dictum "less is more" really applies. Stick to a few plain pieces, avoid decorative twiddles and twirls, aim for understated textures, and you'll actually create a greater impact. Paint walls in a muted matte emulsion and choose flooring for its subtle interest: sisal or coir matting, for example, or perhaps sanded-back (or painted) floorboards with a fake sheepskin rug, or even a low-pile carpet in a color that tones with the walls. Keep your bed frame and all other furniture extremely simple. Minimal, square lines are best, and you might want to invest in one large piece of storage – a wooden chest, for example, or perhaps a long, box-shaped head board with a hinged lid – so that you can hide away anything that's unattractive and non-essential.

◀ A fleece throw and cushions are the focus for a style that's relaxed and modern. Cotton bedlinen makes a lovely contrast, as does the mix of old and new wood, sisal flooring and glass vases.

◀ The raised height of these shelves makes the room seem larger. A fake sheepskin rug on a wooden floor is a classic combination of two wonderful textures.

You can vary the textures in a room such as this by introducing lighter, more translucent objects. Make a drape from a softly gathered length of sheer muslin hung from a metal or bamboo pole, add a paper table lamp or place some colored glass vases on a bedside table. Keep your accessories to a minimum, however – a light touch is best for a bedroom that's both comfortable and contemporary.

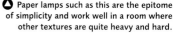

◆ Paper lamps such as this are the epitome of simplicity and work well in a room where other textures are quite heavy and hard.

Sleek and chic

swatch

sleek and chic

In a modern kitchen, metals, stone, and glass make a fabulous combination. Surfaces can vary from rough to smooth, flat to three-dimensional.

Kitchen textures

LAMINATE WORK SURFACE
Dark and mysterious, this marble-effect laminate more than matches its expensive stone competitors.
377

DIMPLED GLASS
The dramatic dimples in this colored glass give it a wonderfully graphic quality. It's ideal for modern cupboard doors.
410

METAL FLOORING
The embossed patterns of metal sheeting makes it a non-slip surface; it also adds another layer of texture to a room.
475

GLASS MOSAIC
Mosaic tiles are often used in bathrooms, but there's no reason why they shouldn't be laid as a kitchen splashback.
437

METAL MESH
A gold-colored metal mesh in a cupboard door panel looks unusual and exciting, with a texture similar to that of knitting.
462

PITTED LIMESTONE
Pale stone floors lighten and brighten small kitchens. Though the slabs can be honed smooth, this rather tough texture is a pleasant antidote to smooth and shiny metal and glass.
529

○ Open shelves and hanging racks are a good way to display kitchenware. Here, smooth stainless steel looks good against matte mosaic tiles.

○ Combining shiny steel with matte paintwork allows both elements to look their best.

◁ A good balance of textural elements gives this kitchen dramatic impact. The dimples on the cupboard doors echo the pierced metal mesh on the drawers.

ONCE THE PRESERVE OF THE PROFESSIONAL KITCHEN, METAL HAS NOW MADE IT INTO EVERYDAY HOMES. TEAM IT WITH PLAIN, PAINTED SURFACES FOR CONTEMPORARY CHIC, OR COMBINE WITH NATURAL WOOD AND STONE FOR A MORE LAID-BACK EFFECT.

The attraction of stainless steel lies in its simplicity and versatility, and it looks particularly lovely in a kitchen that features gentle color. A long run of stainless-steel worktop looks gorgeous, and has a crisp, neat finish that's extremely satisfying. You can take this look further by adding a steel splashback, extractor hood, sink and cooking appliances, and even clever details such as a trim laminated onto the front edge of a shelf. Don't forget that zinc and aluminum are alternatives for a metal splashback. Smaller items, too, from taps to kettles, jugs to containers, can pick up the theme of shiny, metallic surfaces: handles, pulls and switches in a material such as brushed stainless steel are pleasantly tactile. And, if you want to be really adventurous, you could instal a metal floor, or clad the front of your cabinets with a thin sheet of metal.

Natural elements

Vary the textural elements with other ingredients. Stone is an especially good partner – you could choose a limestone, sandstone or slate floor, for example, or a granite or terrazzo worktop, the latter highly polished to echo the reflectivity of metal. For greater contrast, show off the grain of varnished wood, as cupboard fronts or paneling on walls, or perhaps paint units with a pastel shade of matte emulsion. Accessorize with displays of glassware, clear or frosted, crockery in pretty colors and interesting shapes, and bowls of fruit or vases of flowers for a bright finishing touch.

▶ Old-fashioned tea towels with traditional woven patterns have an enduring appeal.

▶ Elegantly plain glassware looks beautiful displayed on a clear glass shelf.

Farmhouse fresh

CHOOSE CLASSIC DESIGNS TO CREATE A KITCHEN THAT'S HOMELY AND COMFORTABLE. ALONGSIDE BARE WOOD, NEAT PAINTWORK AND CERAMIC TILES, ADD SIMPLE GLASSWARE AND OLD-FASHIONED TEA TOWELS TO CREATE A TIMELESS MIX THAT WILL NEVER LET YOU DOWN.

There's a preponderance of wood in this typical farmhouse-style kitchen, but it's been designed with variety in mind: the old wood of the chest of drawers, which is agreeably marked and worn-in, is contrasted with the new wood of the work surface, necessarily smooth and even. The floor is made from boards of a darker wood, which offset the cornflower-blue units. You could achieve this look with pale floorboards by staining or painting them and, if you like the unsophisticated effect of reclaimed wood, search out old pieces of furniture in junk shops, or find a maker who uses reclaimed timber in his or her designs.

Traditional decor

The prettiness of the golden worktops and painted units (low-shine, oil-based eggshell or vinyl silk withstands knocks) is complemented by peach-colored ceramic tiles, which have a gentle sheen and rustic finish completely in keeping with the style of this room. For a slightly more decorative finish, you could choose one-color embossed tiles, or lay plain tiles at 45 degrees for a diagonal pattern.

The solid, hard surfaces of any kitchen benefit from a contrast with lighter, softer textures. Here, translucent glassware has been displayed on open shelves or in cupboards with glass doors; combining open and enclosed storage allows you to show off attractive objects while keeping clutter hidden away. Or display colored crockery, wicker baskets, linen towels or wooden bowls to provide a variety of textures and maintain the simple, farmhouse feel.

swatch

farmhouse fresh

These materials are designed to work together to evoke a particular atmosphere: rustic, informal, and cozy. Their textures are wonderfully varied, which gives the room extra vitality and charm.

Kitchen textures

CERAMIC TILES
Smooth and glossy, ceramic tiles make a good contrast to rougher textures in a farmhouse-style kitchen.
449

RIVEN SLATE
Extremely matte and fairly uneven, this hand-split slate would make an extraordinary kitchen floor.
550

WIRED GLASS
Wired glass instantly conjures up a traditional look and feel. You could use it for cupboard doors, shelves or even a tabletop.
415

STRIPED WEAVE
Plain, striped, or checked fabrics are an ideal choice for this look. This linen-cotton mix has a stripey textural pattern.
178

OAK FLOORING
The ultimate in classic flooring, oak boards have a warm, friendly quality, and an attractive texture and pattern.
505

RAGGED PAINT EFFECT
Rag-rolled paintwork makes a beautiful background for a country-style room.
104

▲ This kitchen's simple style comes from the paneled design of its units, combined with soft colors, natural wood and hand-made ceramic tiles.

▲ A creamy yellow background works well with the textures of old wood, matte metal, traditional glass, ceramic tableware, slate, and a wicker log basket.

Sophisticated dining

◀ Use toning paints as an effective backdrop for hard and soft textures, and dramatic contrasts of color.

Who says walls should always be the same color? The great thing about using paint is that it's inexpensive and easy to apply – and so allows you enormous freedom to experiment with unusual styles and textures.

Paint walls in two, three or more complementary shades and, as shown in the funky, informal dining area to the left, the results can be really impressive. What's more, even though the colors are different, the surface gives one subtle, uniform texture against which to play around with a few dashing contrasts. A warm wool carpet, for example, makes a soft and welcoming flooring, although one could just as easily picture in this environment limed-wood floorboards, natural fiber matting or even groovy rubber.

The furniture is equally striking; wood with metal has a look that's both fashionable and functional, and its square shapes play against the circular pattern of the rug, while the dramatic mix of reflective steel and dark, grainy wood is both sleek and modern.

FOR AN UNHURRIED BREAKFAST, CASUAL LUNCH OR FRIENDLY SUPPER, DECORATE YOUR DINING ROOM WITH RELAXED, SOFT TONES, LETTING A CAREFUL MIX OF INTERESTING TEXTURES PROVIDE AN ATTRACTIVE AND COMFORTABLE BACKGROUND.

Subtle variety

More classic in style, but nevertheless highly appealing, is the simple dining room on the far left, painted in buttermilk yellow with a scrubbed plank floor. The muted blue (and hard, matte texture) of the slate hearth is a lovely complement, as is the pale lilac of the soft pashmina throw that's been casually hung over the back of a dining chair. In fact, the varied textures that have been employed to create this room are so sophisticated they take a while to become apparent: frosted plastic and wire for the modern chandelier, for example; opaque muslin blinds; carved-wood salad servers; a chunky, woven-wicker log basket; clear glass wine goblets; shiny, cream-colored crockery. It's just the sort of delicious, delightful combination that you can enjoy at your leisure over a delicious, relaxing meal with friends or family.

swatch

sophisticated dining

Warm, subtle, and interesting textures are ideal for a dining room that you wish to be contemporary but not aggressive or difficult to live with. Mix a background of smooth paintwork with exotic woods, soft wool carpet, and intriguing fabrics.

Dining room textures

MATTE PAINT
Use matte emulsion as a neutral background, but in a pretty color that complements others in the room.
57

WOOL CARPET
A tufted carpet cut in stripes of two lengths is another way to increase textural interest.
252

EXOTIC WOOD
Rather than choosing a standard wood for furniture or wall panels, you could opt for a stunningly unusual type such as this kevazing veneer.
513

METALLIC SILK
This beautiful fabric is smooth, shiny and extremely elegant. Use it for dining chairs, cushions and drapes.
188

WALLPAPER
Though often patterned, wallpapers can be plain and simple, making an understated textural background.
321

SILK SHEER
A barely-there muslin is a superb ingredient in this type of scheme.
140

Pastel prettiness

WHETHER YOU DECORATE YOUR BATHROOM IN TRADITIONAL OR CONTEMPORARY STYLE, USING A RANGE OF PRETTY, CANDY COLORS WILL ALWAYS ENSURE IT'S A WARM AND WELCOMING HAVEN FOR REFRESHING RELAXATION.

Even with the plainest of fittings you can use color and texture to give a boring bathroom extra interest, while if you're lucky enough to have a statement-making bath or basin they can help to show it off. Take a painted plaster wall as a starting point. Why not add a few rows of shiny ceramic tiles, hand-made so they have a slightly mottled surface and uneven edges – and choose a range of colors that contrast nicely but still look good together? Or you could use vinyl or rubber tiles for a softer, warmer surface, or simply paint a checkerboard of color using small tins of gloss paint. Wood-covered walls, either square panels of M.D.F. or made from tongue-and-groove, can also be painted, in squares or stripes, and there's nothing to stop you continuing your design over the floor as well, if you so wish.

Original thinking

It's this type of lateral thinking that makes the difference between bland and beautiful. Storage, for example, is vital as a means of hiding away all those bathroom bits and pieces, but it doesn't have to be the standard, typical types. You can adapt home office-style units and keep towels in the larger drawers at the bottom with bottles and lotions at the top; or perhaps use wicker baskets, opaque plastic bins, wood and glass cabinets or shiny metal boxes. Pick styles, colors and textures that work with your overall scheme but, at the same time, don't be afraid to use your imagination and have some fun.

▲ Shiny metal, ceramic tiles and laminate drawer fronts: all hard surfaces, but with subtle textural variety.

► Machine-washable cotton bath mats are practical and pleasant to use; the ribbed texture of these examples gives them a nicely three-dimensional quality.

◀ The soft paintwork of this pale-blue wall is a lovely contrast to the hard, shiny tiles. A mottled colorwash paint effect would also have been effective.

▼ Clever, quirky storage ideas are always useful for a bathroom.

pastel prettiness

Think laterally, even when you're on a budget. Pick a range of delicious bubble-gum colors, and vary the textural contrasts from plastic to glass, ceramic to colorwashed paint.

Bathroom textures

342   LINOLEUM FLOORING
This dimpled surface would make a pretty base for an inexpensive bathroom.

381   LAMINATE SURFACE
This type of graphic, abstract pattern would offset plain paintwork and sanitary ware.

447   CERAMIC TILES
The slightly uneven coloring and surface of the tiles add interest.

P.V.C. SHEET
A colored plastic shower curtain can completely transform even the dullest

TEXTURED GLASS
For privacy in a bathroom door or window, or for interesting shelves and

COLORWASH PAINT EFFECT
Jazz up a boring room with an attractive paint

swatch

▲ The smooth, shiny and reflective surfaces in this bathroom give it a sense of luxury and grandeur, but it would not be too difficult to achieve a similar effect yourself.

Mirror, mirror

A LITTLE LUXURY GOES A LONG WAY WHEN YOU USE
MATERIALS THAT ADD A FEELING OF INDULGENCE TO YOUR
BATHROOM. IT'S NOT NECESSARY TO SPEND LOTS OF MONEY,
AS CLEVER THINKING CAN CREATE IMPRESSIVE EFFECTS.

▲ Treat yourself to some expensive soaps and add color and texture to a bathroom.

mirror, mirror

Certain textures create the effect of opulence and indulgence. Make a lasting impression by selecting the surfaces that are stippled, marbled, gilded, and covered in mosaic.

It's all too easy for a modern bathroom to be a flat, lifeless place, but if you can include one or two sumptuous pieces which have glorious texture it will make an enormous difference to the atmosphere.

A fabulous room such as the one on the left, filled with gilding, metal, mirrors and antiques, may not be possible for all of us – but it can still offer some brilliant decorating ideas. The pitted stone floor, for example, looks marvelous against the ultra-smooth, putty-colored walls. If you can't have stone, however, you could substitute reclaimed and limewashed wooden boards, or else use marble-effect linoleum or even imitation-stone vinyl. This will give you a pale (but interesting) base against which everything else in the room will look even more wonderful.

Gorgeous gilding

The huge, cast-iron roll-top bath on the far left is certainly an eye-catching piece, but you can transform the looks of even

Bathroom textures

METALLIC PAINT Spray metallic paint onto junk-shop furniture and the piece will be transformed. For a distressed look, lightly sand the corners once the paint has dried.
96

MARBLE SLAB Cool, hard and smooth, marble is marvelous in a bathroom. This rose-colored example is especially pretty.
562

STIPPLING Stippled walls offer subtle interest. Let one coat of paint dry, then use a stippling brush, textured roller or marine sponge to break up a second coat (in a contrasting color) while it's still wet.
98

MARBLE BRICKS A more intricate but rather understated effect comes from laying marble as brick-shaped flooring.
576

GLASS MOSAIC Small areas of metallic mosaic tiles give dazzling results. For a less intense yet still interesting look, use plain tiles with metallic ones set at random intervals.
427

the most ordinary bath by simply changing the taps. As for the gorgeous gilded chairs, consider scouring junk shops for an old dining chair or two (they needn't match), then try gilding them yourself, or spray paint them with metallic paint. An uneven result is ideal – both charming and full of texture. Then add other second-hand finds such as wash stands with bowls and jugs, mirrors (the more the merrier and, again, you could spray the frames yourself) and intriguing pictures, plus beautiful accessories, from natural sea sponges to luxurious colored and scented soaps.

As a finishing touch, how about changing the handles on drawers or cupboard doors? It's simple enough to do – you just need a little ingenuity. You could, for example, replace dull, ordinary ones with interesting textural types such as seashells or pebbles, rope or leather pulls, cut-glass knobs or stainless-steel bars – the only limit is your imagination.

◀ Cool, hard marble is a wonderful bathroom luxury, and looks fabulous next to the soft sheen of brass and the roughness of a natural sponge.

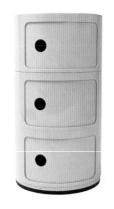

Professional but still personal

MAKE WORKING FROM HOME A PLEASURE RATHER THAN A CHORE BY SURROUNDING YOURSELF WITH FURNITURE AND ACCESSORIES THAT ARE FULL OF CHARACTER, AND USING ONLY COLORS AND TEXTURES THAT YOU REALLY LOVE.

If you're of a fairly-laid back disposition, then your desk, like the one shown right, may be the ideal place for an impromptu stack of colorful paperbacks. At least it gives it a casual appearance that belies its workmanlike functions: drawers full of filing, a large, clear surface and a bright, adjustable lamp.

Deliberate disguise

Sometimes the last thing you want your home office to look like is just that – an office. Painting the walls in a muted color and adding a few favorite objects is the best way to disguise its business-oriented elements. The resulting textural mix will give it a subliminal appeal, too. Even computers these days come in attractive colors, and if you really hate the sight of hi-tech gadgets then you could hide them away, either inside a cupboard (buy one ready-made, or ask a carpenter to make a built-in version) or behind a fold-away screen, perhaps made of wood, paper or frosted glass.

If you've got the space, there's no reason why you shouldn't include a well-padded armchair – or even a couch – for those contemplative moments, with cushions in luxurious velvet, mohair or jumbo cord. Sometimes it's good to question the accepted way of doing things, and not all of us work best when sitting in an office chair. Papers could be stored in woven baskets rather than conventional cardboard files; notebooks could be covered in leather, suede or hand-made paper; then just add paintings, small sculptures, pretty ceramics and, as a finishing touch, a vase of sweet-smelling flowers.

▲ Details make all the difference, and even a tiny touch such as unusual picture frames will add great textural interest.

swatch

professional but still personal

A good variety of pleasant textures makes a noticeable difference to the way that a home office feels. Think of it as a domestic rather than a company-style environment, and include only materials that give you great pleasure and enjoyment.

Home office textures

BIRCH FLOORING
Natural, unpainted wood has an enjoyable grain and texture. A type such as this is unpretentious and helps create a comfortable feel.
521

TEXTURED PAPER
Light and delicate, the texture of paper can lift and brighten a room. Use it for informal lampshades and notebooks.
310

JUMBO CORD
Beautiful fabrics help soften a work room, whatever its style. The fabulous stripes of this jumbo cord would also look good in a living room.
210

TUFTED RUG
A patterned rug adds color and interest; its pleasurable cozy texture is another advantage in a home working space.
245

SOFT SUEDE
You'll appreciate a touch of luxury when you're feeling stressed or stretched at work. Suede, leather, and velvet bring that indulgent feel.
224

TEXTURED GLASS
Use textured glass in a fold-away screen to partition your room for privacy, yet still keep a light, airy feel.
406

▲ If you want to create a characterful office, choose clever storage such as these circular plastic stacking units.

◗ This unconventional home office contains a gentle mix of appealing textures, from the natural wood of the desk to the chrome and glass lamp, and the leather-covered books.

making a home office work

Bear in mind that a combination of color, texture, and pattern can make even the most inexpensive of materials interesting and attractive.

Home office textures

PATTERNED GLASS
Use toughened, textured glass for an unusual, see-through desktop rested on simple trestle legs.

409

SMOOTH P.V.C
Smooth plastic often has groovy, saturated color and makes a bright, bold statement.

353

LINOLEUM FLOORING
Inexpensive, durable and easy-to-clean, this flooring features statement-making graphic embossed disks.

345

WOOL CARPET
A neutral-colored carpet can provide a good base if you're planning to inject spots of color elsewhere.

254

CHIPBOARD
Although usually painted over, you may prefer chipboard's interesting texture when left bare.

519

Making a home office work

◀ Wood, glass, and plastic combine for an inexpensive but highly efficient and texturally interesting workspace.

▼ The roll-top front of this prettily colored melamine storage cabinet minimizes space yet allows easy access to files.

Why make life complicated? A thick sheet of strengthened glass laid securely on two painted or unpainted wood (or metal) trestle legs may be all you need as your home office desk. Not only is it large, stable and level, it's also good-looking and easy to use.

You can then base your scheme around the contrast of glass and metal or glass and wood, adding some open shelving units, chests of drawers or simple individual shelves fixed to the walls. Your chair could, similarly, be made of metal or wood, while a desk lamp might have a wooden base with frosted glass shade, or be in the form of a metal hinged-arm light. If you wish, consider adding another texture with either matte or shiny plastic: it's both practical and inexpensive for chairs, lights, or storage units and accessories such as fans, pen holders and filing trays, and comes in a wide variety of pretty colors.

Trade tips

The simplest treatment for walls is to paint them a muted, matte background color – though shiny gloss paint would be extra hard-wearing as an alternative. Or you could use blackboard paint – ideal for a home office or a child's room – on which you could write and wipe messages and memos. A fantastically useful and visually interesting addition would be to screw a large steel sheet to the wall to act as a magnetic notice board. And a cheap finishing touch would be magazine files made of cardboard. If you're really short of money, there's nothing wrong with using old shoe boxes (cover them in wrapping paper if you want a more finished effect) or painted fruit crates as an unusual means of storage.

SETTING UP A HOME OFFICE CAN SOMETIMES BE AN EXPENSIVE BUSINESS – BUT IT DOESN'T HAVE TO BE SO. IF YOU CHOOSE YOUR FURNISHINGS CAREFULLY THEY CAN BE BOTH FUNCTIONAL AND ATTRACTIVE, WITHOUT COSTING A FORTUNE.

◗ A whimsical plastic floor fan adds an element of fun to working from home.

Strong

BOLD, **BRIGHT** COLOURS ARE INVIGORATING, **DRAMATIC** AND SOPHISTICATED. THEY MAKE A **SUPERB** PARTNER FOR TEXTURES WITH **CHARACTER**, RESULTING IN ROOMS THAT NEVER FAIL TO **IMPRESS**.

colors

STRONG COLORS

Any decorating scheme that uses strong colors is bound to make a big impression. However eye-catching strong colors are, though, they don't have to be brash or unpleasantly bright – clever thinking can create rooms that are interesting and involving without being horribly over the top.

Many people think of bold colors as being just the three primaries: red, yellow and blue. Splashes of these can look fantastic (think of Chinese red lacquered boxes or brilliant blue glass), but when used over large areas they are best suited to a children's bedroom or playroom. Consider, instead, other strong colors that will appear more sophisticated: they work well in families, such as aubergine, claret, midnight blue, and bottle green; spicy tones such as red ochre, mustard, cinnamon, and saffron; or Mediterranean shades such as sea blue, yellow, or aquamarine.

Start by just using one bold color, perhaps surrounded by neutrals, and if you're feeling daring add one or two others in a complementary shade. Be careful with contrasts – small doses are best, or you'll end up with a busy, clamorous room in which every color is competing for attention.

Strong color schemes are more versatile than you might think. They can often, for example, create a wonderful ethnic or global style, with the use of dyed raffia, tin ornaments, sheer or opaque fabrics (perhaps with a metallic weave), paper wall hangings, and woven rugs. Or, when used with appropriate furnishings, they can suggest a historical style such as Georgian, Victorian, or even '50s or '60s. And they can be highly contemporary, incorporating funky, fun textures from rubber and plastic to colored acrylic and fiber-optic fabrics.

Perhaps the most important thing to bear in mind when using bold colors is that they shouldn't overpower the textures you have chosen. Get the best from strong colors by treating them in a measured, thoughtful way, and they will enhance a textural scheme to truly stunning effect.

VIVID, SPICY REDS ARE REMINISCENT OF
AFRICA AND INDIA – USE WARM WOOL AND SOFT
COTTON TO OFFSET THE GLAMOROUS SHIMMER OF
SILK FOR A SUMPTUOUS AND DRAMATIC SCENE.

Global influence

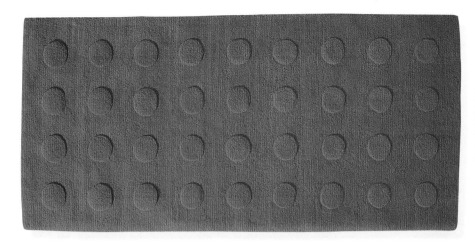

A three-dimensional pile is a subtle touch on a searingly bright tufted rug: it would be best used in a fairly large, uncluttered room alongside a few bold, ethnic accessories.

The accessories in this room – a clear glass vase, white ceramic bowl and basketware plant holder – have been kept quite plain so as not to detract from the vitality of the fabrics.

Instead of using paint, why not cover a wall with a hanging made from inexpensive fabric, or even paper? The textural effect, as shown here, is amazing.

Eastern-style piles of floor cushions make a modern statement in a living room, and are a great way to create textural contrast – you can use as many different fabrics as you like, simply linking them by color, shape and graduating size. Even if you're on a budget, you might be able to find small remnants of expensive or unusual fabric which will lift your scheme no end.

You can vary the look by adding all sorts of fabulous trimmings: ribbon, beading, raffia, sequins, rows of buttons, ric-rac, even feathers. Each cushion can be made from two or more types of material: go for the ultimate in contrast with, say, linen next to velvet, organza layered over satin, or perhaps sari fabric with plain cotton. The same goes for drapes, too. The main picture shows how thick, heavy wool drapes have been given a quirky, scalloped trim. An edging made of velvet or linen would have been equally attractive, or perhaps a deep border along the bottom in vibrant red felt.

Ethnic accents

As much as fabrics, your choice of accessories will help shape the style of the room, whether they be oriental red lacquer boxes, embossed brass trays from India or painted African gourds. If you want to keep the look fairly low-key, however, stick to furniture, walls and floors in plain, subtle shapes and materials. In this contemporary room, for example, white walls and a relatively plain white couch have been teamed with a simple metal and marble coffee table and a natural wool carpet, creating a neutral background that allows touches of bold color and texture to be seen at their best.

Moody blues

A DARING USE OF ONE STRONG COLOR CAN HAVE ENORMOUS IMPACT – IT LOOKS ESPECIALLY GOOD WHEN MIXED WITH THE NATURAL BEAUTY OF GRAINY WOOD, RUGGED STONE, AND HAIRY COIR.

▲ A chenille-covered couch offers subtle textural interest, especially when teamed with cushions trimmed with piping. A mohair or felt throw would add a soft touch.

One way to approach a living room scheme is by thinking of it in terms of layers. Start with the floor – to create the look of a room like the one to the right, place a large natural fiber mat (coir, seagrass, sisal or rush) over a stone floor. These tiles are made of terracotta, but limestone, sandstone or perhaps even concrete slabs would work equally well.

The contrast of these two textures is a good way to begin, and can be built upon with the wall treatment – perhaps smooth paintwork, as here, or a rougher plaster finish, or maybe paper-backed hessian for an earthy, rustic effect. This room has the advantage of an interesting ceiling, too. If you're lucky enough to have exposed wooden beams, you could leave them bare, stain them, or paint them to match your color scheme.

Finishing touches

Window treatments add another layer. Here, a simple approach has been taken, with unbleached linen in informal gathers and tied back with an oversized woven tassel – it's an echo of the rough-and-smooth floor treatment and is both easy and inexpensive to achieve. Furniture and accessories are your final layer. Large pieces made from sustainable tropical hardwood look good in this room, though old pine would be just as attractive, as would a combination of stone and metal. The couch and chairs manage to be both smart and comfortable, and a few pieces of glassware in toning colours complete the look superbly.

moody blues

With strong colors, a balanced mix of textures is vital. Combine hard and soft, rough and smooth, hairy and silky, opaque and sheer, to result in a room that has unquestionable appeal.

Living room textures

315 **HESSIAN WALLCOVERING**
This has a subtle texture that would complement both rough and smooth surfaces.

153 **TEXTURED SHEER**
An unusual fabric that adds interest when used for blinds or other soft furnishings.

413 **PATTERNED GLASS**
Use for a coffee table top, a cupboard door, or an uplit shelf.

577 **TERRACOTTA FLOOR TILE**
Old terracotta floor tiles have a delightful patina that makes an excellent base for a room. Top with a rug for softness.

172 **SMOOTH COTTON**
Workmanlike cotton is inexpensive, easy to clean, and long-lasting.

288 **SISAL/FLAX FLOORING**
This flooring is relatively neutral, but has a subtle texture.

swatch

▼ Candles in interesting colors are an attractive accessory, even when unlit.

◀ The textural scheme has been built up layer by layer in this airy room for a relaxing balance of hard and soft, rough and smooth, clear and opaque.

flame shades

Don't compete with bold colors by using too many surfaces. Variety is good, but choose calm, smooth textures like oak, leather, and glass.

Living room textures

SANDBLASTED GLASS
Glass can be smooth and matte, or highly polished, with unusual patterns and contrasts of opacity and clarity.
401

SMOOTH COTTON
Smooth cotton is practical and useful – it will complement almost every other material without detracting from them.
171

TEXTURED CHENILLE
The warm, inviting texture of chenille is soft and giving, making a pleasant change from harder, colder surfaces.
205

PIERCED LEATHER
Leather, though sophisticated, is fairly unobtrusive, and will work well in any type of room scheme.
227

OAK FLOORBOARDS
The satiny, shiny surface of oak, with its beautiful grained pattern, makes an excellent choice for an upmarket and attractive floor.
499

LIMESTONE SLAB
While limestone is essentially cold and smooth, its slightly rough surface is full of character and perfectly complements the softer textures of fabric.
528

Flame shades

WARM, VIBRANT AND WELCOMING, SPLASHES OF BRILLIANT RED OR ORANGE ADD A TOUCH OF DRAMA TO A LIVING ROOM. COMBINE WITH RELAXED NEUTRALS AND THE RESULT IS A SCHEME THAT'S INSTANTLY UPLIFTING.

▼ An unconventional color combines with an unusual texture to make this seating unique and eye-catching.

◀ Silk in shades from tangerine to magenta makes ideal scatter cushions or even imposing drapes.

◀ This rug makes a dramatic centerpiece to a room which is otherwise filled with the neutral colors and natural textures of leather, stone, brick, metal, and wood.

When attempting a dramatic color scheme, it's best to do a fair amount of research and preparation first. Tear pages out of magazines, brush sample pots of paint onto walls and pin fabric swatches together, until you've got a clear feel for what you're doing. Allow one color to dominate, perhaps using others as accents. Or, for a more low-key look, team just one strongly colored piece (a rug, couch, or painting, for example) with surroundings in beautiful neutrals.

Colorful effects

Creating an eye-catching living room, for example, is easy if you choose seating in brilliant colors such as the orange couches and chairs shown on the bottom left. The key is to let such a vivid color make its impact without distraction, by keeping everything else in the room subtle and undemanding. Here, walls are plain white and the floor a simple wood that has a gentle sheen, while the glass coffee table and slender, metal and plastic lamp are so understated as to be almost invisible. What's more, all these smooth, hard surfaces make an effective textural contrast to the unusual ruched effect of the fabric seat covers.

In a cozy sitting room like the one on the top left, a red, yellow and black rug becomes the focal point in front of a glowing fire. Its tufted surface happily combines with the other textures in the room – smooth leather, pitted stone, rough metal, crunchy linen, and grained wood – and its inviting color demonstrates how these shades can be used successfully in settings that range from the ultra-modern to the typically traditional.

◀ A plastic chair in tomato red could be used for occasional seating or in a home office. Wherever it's placed, it will certainly make a statement.

All-out glamor

WHEN YOU WANT TO GIVE THAT BOUDOIR
FEEL TO A BEDROOM, COMBINE VIBRANT SHADES
OF PINK AND RED WITH THE LUXURIOUS TEXTURES
OF SILK AND VELVET, THROWING IN TASSELS,
GILT AND QUILTING FOR ADDED IMPACT.

However much you love strong colors, they're not always the most restful choice for a bedroom – though they can work wonderfully as vivid accents in a room that's otherwise fairly neutral. On the right, for example, a sky-blue quilted eiderdown with vivid pink flowers makes a dramatic focal point for a bed that's covered in cool, calm ivory and oyster-colored fabrics. The fabulous texture of quilted silk subtly links the bold and the understated shades, while in the background the intricate carving of the oversized wooden door is nicely complementary; it also provides a hard, rough texture to counterpoint the luxurious softness everywhere else in the room.

▶ This pretty bedroom contrasts
rough and smooth, sheer and
opaque, hard and soft. The pink
is saved from being overpowering
by the plentiful use of white.

Impressive ingenuity

This effect can be emulated relatively easily, by choosing plain white or off-white bed linen and simply adding a brightly colored eiderdown, bedcover or throw in suitably luxurious fabric: perhaps silk satin, like in this opulent room, or else mohair, cashmere, soft wool, velvet or even pashmina. If your budget won't stretch to brand-new, ready-made textiles, look for discounted ends of lines or remnants, or check out second-hand shops or jumble sales for pieces that could be washed, cut up and adapted – you may only need a smallish square to make a central panel around which you could sew a plain border.

These smooth, soft textures can be nicely contrasted with a bare wooden floor, roughly plastered walls or carved wooden mirrors or picture frames. A lamp with a branch-like wooden base – as seen in the bedroom above left – some pieces of hand-thrown pottery or a couple of woven storage baskets would all be ideal additions to this look. Or, if you want a more feminine, film-star style, choose pieces such as the Parisian-style metal chair below right, with its plush upholstery and tasseled fringe. Alternatively, you could add gilded picture frames, antique engraved glass goblets, assorted candle-holders and maybe even an eccentric lampshade made of plastic, taffeta or feathers.

swatch

all-out glamor

These textures have been chosen for their no-holds-barred, glamorous effect: linen, chenille, taffeta, a tufted sheer, and an exotic zebra-skin print. Ensure, however, that you give soft fabrics a counterpoint by using harder surfaces as well.

Bedroom textures

ROUGH PLASTER
Offset luxurious fabrics with a few harder, rougher surfaces such as this unevenly applied plaster.

481

NATURAL LINEN
Crisp and clean, with a noticeable weave, pure linen is unmistakably smart and elegant.
185

FAKE ZEBRA SKIN
Place a dramatic fake zebra skin on the floor or over a bed as the focal point of a boudoir-style bedroom.

230

CRUNCHY TAFFETA
Delicate and pretty taffeta is an ideal choice when you're aiming for a highly feminine room scheme.
218

SOFT CHENILLE
This gorgeously soft, unevenly woven texture complements the fabric's deeply saturated raspberry pink color.

204

TUFTED COTTON SHEER
These soft bobbles add fun and interest to what could otherwise be a fairly uninteresting fabric.

144

▲ The opulent effect of quilting on a silk-satin fabric is emphasized by the use of a bright splash of color and also by the rough hardness of the wooden door.

◀ This junk-shop chair with its raffish elegance and air of '50s Paris would add plenty of character to a boudoir-style bedroom.

▲ A range of colors and carefully selected textures ensures the success of this inviting bedroom.

Color crazy

WHEN NOTHING BUT THE BRIGHTEST BEDROOM WILL
DO, USE VIBRANT SHADES AND SOPHISTICATED
TEXTURES TO CREATE A TRULY DRAMATIC IMPACT.

Danish designer Verner Panton once said that one sits more comfortably on a color that one likes. The same could be said for sleeping, bathing, eating, working ... . In fact, if you enjoy color there's no reason why you shouldn't have fun using it throughout your home.

Wild at heart

To create an exuberant, appealing color mix, start by choosing a theme – which may be just one color range or a combination of shades that work well together – and ensure that your textural contrasts are fairly subtle: too much texture as well as color could be over-the-top. In the light-filled bedroom on the left, the colors chosen are very varied – lime green, pink, cornflower blue, lilac, orange and yellow – but all have a similar depth of tone (there are no pastels or dark shades) and a lovely Mediterranean-style freshness. What's more, they're limited to the bed frame, bed linen, chair and lamps, all of which have a plain, smooth texture. The floor has been chosen for its neutral color and texture; the main surface interest is the rough, uneven wall, painted a contrasting bright white to offset the room's contents.

In the vivid pink bedroom on the right, by comparison, the colors are less varied and the textures more so: smooth painted wood and walls have been teamed with soft, frilly lace, hard, shiny glass and the feathery trim of the coat hanging beside the bed. Not everyone would welcome such intensity of color, but it does work, thanks to a thoughtful use of texture and a willingness to be a little different.

◑ A plastic tie-back is an unusual choice, but here it perfectly complements the bold colors of the drapes themselves.

◑ There's a definite sense of theatricality to this room; the intensity of the hot pink is offset by an enjoyable variety of textures.

color crazy

Use texture to emphasize and complement a bold and bright color scheme. Choose lace and sheers, smooth linoleum, glass, and fluffy fur to create a bedroom with personality and attitude.

Bedroom textures

154 **LAYERED SHEER**
Three layers of light, sheer polyester in different colors – perfect for an unusual blind.

157 **LACE**
Old-fashioned lace is a wonderful addition to bedroom, whether the look is classic or more eclectic.

347 **LINOLEUM FLOORING**
An unusual idea for a bedroom, you could also use lino with a textured pattern.

399 **COLORED GLASS**
A smooth, matte, colored glass would look calm and quiet in a bedroom with plenty of color and texture.

362 **ACRYLIC SHEETING**
Intensely colored smooth plastic with a laid-back texture.

239 **LAMBSKIN**
Indulge yourself with a furry rug or throw – it's three-dimensional and very tactile.

swatch

▲ A combination of simple textures is all that's needed when using such a striking color scheme.

Simple intensity

THE BOLD TONES OF SCARLET, CRIMSON, MAUVE AND PURPLE INDICATE INTIMACY, LUXURY AND OPULENCE. REALLY VIVID COLORS SUCH AS THESE CAN SUCCEED IN A BEDROOM IF YOU HAVE THE CONFIDENCE TO TAKE A NO-HOLDS-BARRED APPROACH.

When making a daring statement, it's generally best to choose relatively uncomplicated textures. The smooth wall in the room above, for example, is offset by a lovely rough coir floorcovering in an unusual pale color, and the fabrics on the bed are straightforward linen, velvet and quilted nylon, with no fancy borders, trims, buttons or tassels. Every piece in the room has a simple, graphic quality, and that extends particularly to the furniture, which demonstrates strong, pared-down shapes and clean lines – it makes a

 A screen is a useful addition to a bedroom; here, it's covered in a soft, warm fabric which contrasts nicely with the stone floor, while mirroring the armchair and silky cushions.

 An assortment of strong colors makes this inexpensive bed linen stand out in a stylish statement against the pale walls.

quiet but effective statement that's ideal in this scheme. It's best, after that, to select just a couple of additional colors around which to base your design, either from the same "family", or to create an unexpected contrast. (How about khaki with scarlet, bottle green with brilliant orange, or navy with lemon yellow? Experiment with fabric swatches and sample paints before committing yourself.) The alternative is to paint walls white and say it all with colored bed linen: a versatile solution, especially if you buy a variety of sets and mix them to provide an interesting rainbow of colors.

Brilliant brushwork

For the utmost impact with minimum effort and expense, take the simple option of painting just one wall of a bedroom in a vital, intense color. Matte emulsion will have softness and depth, while gloss will look more sophisticated; or you could try an unusual paint such as suede-effect, pearlescent, or even glitter. Choose your shade carefully; it must be one you can live with, and with which you can coordinate bed linen, furniture and accessories without too much difficulty.

simple intensity

Strong but straightforward textures make a clear statement. Team them with a range of bold, contrasting colors and furniture that's been chosen for its graphically pared-down shape.

Bedroom textures

RAG RUG This modern take on the traditional rag rug has a gorgeous soft, fluffy texture and would be ideal beside a bed.	**248**	**JUMBO CORD** Softly ribbed jumbo cord is perfect for upholstering a bedside chair, or even making a cozy throw or cushion cover.	**209**
CHERRY WOOD The deep color and very definite grain of cherry wood gives it a vital and luxurious appearance.	**510**	**METALLIC SILK** The delicate, shiny surface of this light silk has been shot through with metallic threads, giving it a texture that's subtle yet interesting.	**189**

▶ Bedroom lighting often has great decorative appeal and can be used to reinforce or contrast with a textural theme.

IT CAN BE HARD TO FIND THE RIGHT SCHEME FOR A TEENAGER'S ROOM, BUT A MIX OF STRONG SHADES IS A GOOD START. THEN PICK INEXPENSIVE, INFORMAL FURNISHINGS AND A RANGE OF APPEALING ACCESSORIES FOR A LOOK THAT'S BOTH TRENDY AND ACHIEVABLE.

Young and fun

swatch

young and fun

Use textures that have strong definition for a confident scheme. Their contrasting surfaces will contribute to the effect when used with a range of complementary colors.

Bedroom textures

KNITTING
Knitted cushion covers or throws are easy to make yourself: if you can't knit, chop up an old sweater, and seam it together.
123

COTTON SHEER
A gauzy window hanging is pretty and practical, allowing light to filter through while also retaining privacy.
143

SHEEPSKIN
The long, three-dimensional pile of fluffy sheepskin is incredibly soft and tactile. It works extremely well on top of wooden floorboards.
237

PATTERNED GLASS
Glass like this adds interest to an exterior window, or could be used equally well for a wardrobe door.
411

WOOL CARPET
This carpet has the look of a natural fiber flooring, but is in fact made of softer wool, so would be ideal in a bedroom.
267

ROUGH PLASTER
A textured-plaster wall finish provides a dramatic background to a bedroom, with other textures being kept relatively plain.
488

In a bedroom based around bold colors, a few statement-making pieces will really pull the look together. It could be bed linen or cushions, a radio or a light, or maybe some special storage boxes. In this bright bedroom, for instance, lemon yellow is offset against two shades of pink to create an eye-catching color scheme. Just as important, however, is the pleasant range of textures, which are easy-going and also interesting.

It all starts with the wooden floorboards, which have been given a wash with thinned-down paint so that the grain still shows through – the result being more "finished" than bare boards but still natural in appearance. The timber theme continues with a slatted futon bed base and folding side table, both unpainted and unpretentious; together, however, these elements provide the basics for an attractive scheme that could be emulated quickly, easily, and cheaply.

Making an impact

The real scene-stealers in the room, though, are the duvet and cushion covers, in an unmissable range of pretty pinks and a gorgeous variety of textures. The duvet cover has been appliquéd with daisies – a lovely way to jazz up a plain piece of fabric – and the knitted cushions are finished with bobbled, waffle and appliquéd surfaces, themselves a contrast to the smooth knitted throw that's been laid neatly over the end of the bed. The sheer muslin curtain adds another textural layer, while the whole room is completed with the scattering of a few fashionable accessories made from rough, hairy sisal, and smooth, shiny glass and plastic.

◀ Instantly update a plain room by using bright bed linen and painting spacious boxes in complementary shades.

▲ The colors of this pretty room are what first make an impression, but its textures have been well thought through, too.

DARK WOOD AND GLEAMING METAL MAKE STUNNING
PARTNERS. THESE ROOMS ARE BASED AROUND AN INTERESTING
JUXTAPOSITION OF HARD TEXTURES AND STRONG COLORS.

Dark and dramatic

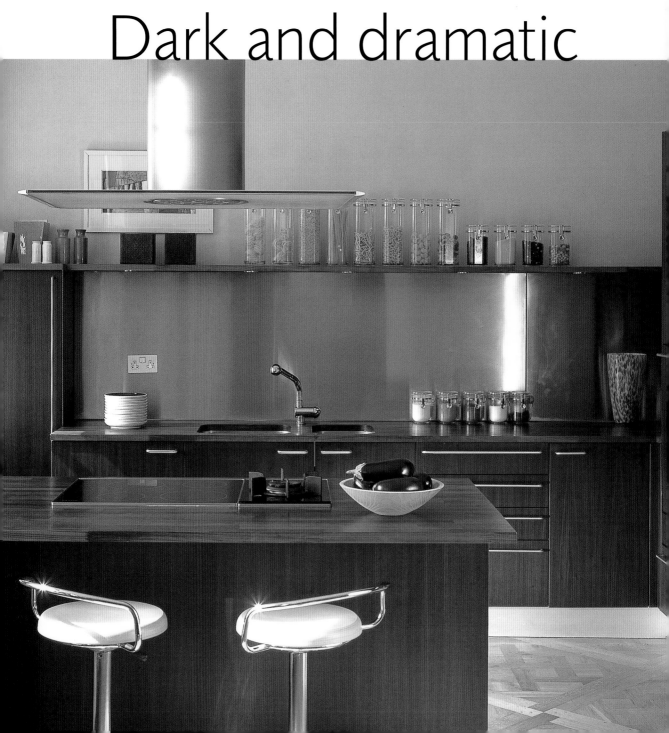

This roughly plastered wall makes a fabulous background to the smoothness of the storage unit – it's a nice way to tone down the sometimes stark feel of a modern kitchen.

Modern cutlery and a sculptural glass bowl have a fresh, striking look – perfect with bold colors, metal and exotic woods.

swatch

dark and dramatic

The hard surfaces of a kitchen provide an ideal opportunity to experiment with interesting textures, colors, and patterns.

Kitchen textures

LAMINATE WORK SURFACE
This mysterious, metallic pattern would add vitality even to a relatively plain kitchen.
371

LINOLEUM FLOORING
Lino can imitate various other materials, including aluminum treadplate. Excellent for a kitchen with vigor and verve.
348

GLASS MOSAIC
These sleek mosaic tiles are dazzling in their variety. Their metallic colors and subtly different textures are unusual and eye-catching.
426

MAHOGANY
Very dark woods are fabulous teamed with shiny metal – the combination of their colors and textures gives a glamorous, modern look.
495

An unusual, dark wood makes a dramatic impact in a small kitchen: the example on the left uses walnut, although other exotic yet sustainable types would also be suitable. Plain and simple, the large expanses of cupboard doors are nicely contrasted with a parquet floor made from antique oak, its surface scratched, dented and marked. Completing the picture is a counter top also made from dark wood.

If you have wall units, it's a good idea to hang fluorescent strips beneath them to light your working areas, hiding their glare with a baffle (thin strip of wood) in front. A large panel of stainless steel will help to magnify light, and in this kitchen, reflective metal makes a secondary theme, from the splashback and the extractor hood to the elongated door handles and the bar stools. The final theme is one of glass: at the base of the extractor and in the rows of highly practical storage jars.

The unfitted kitchen

As an alternative to a fully fitted room you could choose several free-standing storage-cum-preparation units. A wooden butcher's block evokes a traditional style, while contemporary, streamlined designs are reminiscent of European homes. Look for details such as wheels or interesting handles, and use the flexibility that this type of kitchen gives you to make the most of other features in your scheme – perhaps a special wall finish, a table lamp, or a treasured piece of art or craft.

Strong horizontal and vertical lines in this kitchen are emphasized by the long handles on the wooden units. The whole scheme has been carefully thought through and looks ultra-sophisticated.

▶ The bold orange of these plastic chairs is nicely offset by pale pine and shiny metal.

▼ Glass has great potential, as the dimpled surface of this table demonstrates.

Making an impact

PICK ONE VIBRANT COLOR FOR YOUR KITCHEN OR DINING AREA AND
ADD DASHES OF COMPLEMENTARY SHADES. THIS NO-HOLDS-BARRED
APPROACH IS SPIRITED, CHEERFUL AND UPLIFTING TO LIVE WITH.

making an impact

Using simple, relatively plain textures is a good idea when your aim is to complement a strong color scheme. Ensure that they're interesting without being distracting or interfering.

Kitchen textures

79 MATTE EMULSION
Kitchen cupboards made of cheap wood can be transformed by bright paint.

410 DIMPLED GLASS
Though clear and relatively unobtrusive, this glass makes a strong impression.

387 LAMINATE SURFACE
A man-made surface can also look good and is cheaper than stone.

538 PINK GRANITE
Granite makes a marvelous kitchen work surface – cool, hard, and very distinctive in appearance.

526 LIMESTONE SLAB
A stone floor, such as this limestone slab, will last forever. It's subtle and sophisticated, though not cheap.

514 TROPICAL HARDWOOD
Wood has a gentler, warmer texture than that of stone or glass.

swatch

In a kitchen that's dominated by one bold color, it's really important to get the other elements right. Floors, walls and worksurfaces in natural shades are often the best choice (the floor of the kitchen shown below, for example, is made of honed limestone and the worktop is highly polished pink granite), though sometimes picking out a complementary or contrasting color will work – with small insets in patterned lino, for example, or the border to a tiled splashback. Here a white wall, covered in matte emulsion, echoes the matte surface of the painted unit doors; it's the different degrees of matte and luster that add enormous, though subtle, interest to this room.

On the shelf

The centerpiece of this kitchen is the impressive stainless-steel cooker and its extractor hood, flanked by two wall cupboards with doors made of glass and steel. Not only do the latter pull the look together, they also allow an intriguing glimpse of all the bright kitchen bits that have been stored inside. These days, cooking gadgets come in all sorts of glorious colors, so it's possible to transform even the dullest of kitchens with an inexpensive new kettle, juicer, food processor, or whisk.

The same is true of dining areas, too: a neutral table – perhaps made of glass and metal, inexpensive pine, or a classic, dark hardwood – makes a versatile centerpiece for chairs in any color or material you like, whether they be upholstered in velvet or canvas, made from plastic and metal, or in bare or painted wood. Add a table runner, some plants or flowers, mats, crockery, napkins and glasses, in one bold color or varying candy colors, and you'll easily create a characterful, irresistible setting.

▼ This kitchen has plenty of color and quite a lot on display: note how the large floor slabs provide a clean, uncomplicated base for this look.

Over the rainbow

WITH A LITTLE COURAGE AND A DASH OF PANACHE, YOU CAN USE STRONG
COLORS TO CREATE AN EXCITING – AND INEXPENSIVE – SCHEME.

◀ In the background of the dining room on the far left, the living room wall was created by mixing purple pigment with the plaster, then coating with yacht varnish when it was dry.

◀ The simple, straightforward materials used in this room offer a range of attractive textures that pleasantly offset the bold lilac of the wall.

Painting walls, ceiling and woodwork in vibrant colors is a cheap, quick and easy way to transform the character of a room. Bold tones can work particularly well in a dining area, where you want to create an atmosphere of friendliness, vibrancy and expectation that's conducive to enjoyable meals. If you've decided to take the plunge and mix more than one shade, think carefully about which colors will work together. Look at those that come from a similar family – cool, warm, spicy, pastels, or primaries, for example – and if in doubt be inspired by the graduating shades used in the paint charts at any good hardware store. For extra textural effect, vary the finish from matte to satin to gloss; even with a restricted color palette this will make a great deal of difference.

When choosing fabrics, pick out one or two of your paint colors or use a limited range of neutrals with a down-to-earth feel such as white muslin, unbleached linen or artist's canvas; there does come a point when too much color is overwhelming, and simple, soft textures can help tone everything down.

A calming influence

Always try to maintain a balance: strongly colored or textured areas need to be mitigated by others that are plainer and easier to live with. In these dining areas, for example, while strong tones predominate, the floors and tables are made of plain, unpretentious materials, and the overall effect owes a lot to the light and airy nature of each of the rooms. Accessories have been kept to a minimum and carefully co-ordinated in limited colors – though the owner of the dining room on the far left loves bold colors so much that she couldn't resist adding a set of plastic dining chairs in a variety of pretty shades.

swatch

over the rainbow

When you're using several strong shades in one room, ensure that textures are varied but also balanced. Too many funky or dramatic surfaces will only clamor for attention and clash unpleasantly.

Dining room textures

CANVAS FABRIC
Tough canvas fabric is versatile and durable. Its quiet texture will offset more glamorous surfaces.
214

MOTTLED WALLPAPER
Marbled wallpaper makes an interesting back-ground without being overly dramatic.
333

THICK FELT
Warm, fuzzy felt is a pleasant fabric for an informal dining room and comes in an impressive variety of bold colors.

316

CHESTNUT WOOD
The natural patina and soft sheen of wood makes a calming contribution to a scheme such as this.

500

swatch

blue heaven

Use layers of texture to complement strong colors, from linoleum on the floor to wallpaper, unusual paint effects, and mosaic tiles.

Bathroom textures

RUBBER MAT
Dimpled rubber has a three-dimensional texture for good grip and an appealing look – great for colorful bath mats.

344

GLASS MOSAIC
Tiny mosaic tiles come in gorgeous saturated colors. Some have a pleasantly uneven, hand-finished texture, as here.

431

PAINT EFFECT
This paint effect only needs a plain white suite and minimal accessories to be the basis for an inspiring bathroom.

118

LINOLEUM FLOORING
As a base for a characterful, colorful room, this textured lino would be hard to beat.

349

CORK FLOOR TILE
Warm and soft under-foot, yet tough and waterproof, cork makes an excellent textured bathroom flooring.

303

TEXTURED WALLPAPER
A subtly textured wallpaper can form an excellent background to bold colors and more noticeable surfaces.

323

 An interesting bathroom can easily be created with little expense but a certain amount of ingenuity. Here, a variety of textures and bold use of color give the room strong character.

◀ Mosaic creates a splash of vivid color and three-dimensional texture. It's not even very difficult to make yourself.

Bathroom furniture often tends to be straightforward and simple, especially when it's of the less expensive type. You can, however, create a beautifully designed and well-thought-through room based around even the plainest of plain white suites.

Inexpensive ideas

Start by considering either the walls or the floor. The cheapest and easiest option is to paint the walls a wonderful, strong color – blue or green always looks good in a bathroom, though you may prefer to choose something different – and then lay a water-resistant flooring in either a complementary or a neutral shade.

Bearing in mind the textures of your walls and floor, you can now start to build up other areas of the room bit by bit. Tiny mosaic tiles help to break up expanses of hard, smooth surfaces, and lend themselves well to areas of intense color. If you can't afford to cover a whole wall in them, you could easily (as shown in the bright bathroom opposite) create a small basin splashback, or perhaps a mirror surround, or a picture frame.

Another choice for frames, or maybe a medicine cabinet, would be plain wood, perhaps with a limed or distressed paint finish. Other storage might consist of glass shelves (good for creating an illusion of lightness and space) and plastic baskets, in bright colors that suit those of the walls and floor. Each of these elements provides another pleasurable texture, while towels, which offer a welcoming soft and fluffy contrast, can be hung from rails or hoops, or stored folded or rolled in shelves, boxes or baskets. And, as a finishing touch, add some houseplants, colored rubber mats and plastic or glass bottles containing your favorite lotions and potions.

Blue heaven

TAKE A GORGEOUS WASH OF COLOR AS YOUR BATHROOM STARTING POINT, ADDING ACCESSORIES IN COMPLEMENTARY SHADES AND INTERESTING TEXTURES. PUT IT TOGETHER LAYER BY LAYER AND THE RESULT WILL BE A ROOM WITH PERSONALITY AND PANACHE.

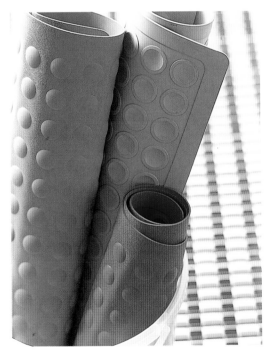

◀ Dimpled rubber adds a pleasant texture and color, and is ideal for bath mats.

Bathing beauties

BATHROOM FURNITURE IN CLEAN, STRUCTURAL SHAPES AND SIMPLE LINES WORKS WELL WITH BOLD COLORS, WHETHER THE OVERALL STYLE IS CLASSIC, CONTEMPORARY OR A MIXTURE OF THE TWO.

There's a certain timeless elegance to reclaimed stone flags that makes them the perfect choice as a flooring for both traditional and modern bathrooms. They're a great complement to the smoothness of the other elements of the room, maybe because they're slightly rough around the edges. And if you find the idea of stepping out of the bath onto a stone floor a little chilling, there's always the option of underfloor heating.

Painted wooden floorboards are a less expensive alternative to a stone floor - several layers of floor paint covered with marine varnish should make them suitably waterproof. Contrast with a wall painted in a definite color, with a solid finish or perhaps colorwashed, dragged or stippled. You could clad the wall in an interesting material: tongue-and-groove timber and ceramic tiles are both traditional, but you could also use tiny mosaic tiles, panels of painted and varnished M.D.F., or wall tiles made of marble or slate.

For further textural impact, there's a wealth of different materials available: baths could be a cast-iron roll-top version, enameled pressed steel, acrylic or even stainless steel, while basins could be made of glass, stone or wood instead of the conventional ceramic. That's not to mention unfitted pieces and accessories where there are, of course, endless possibilities.

A lasting impression

The key to a successful bathroom of this type, however, is in your choice of furniture, both fitted and free-standing. Think of shapes that are clean and simple, and individual pieces that make an impact. Select strong lines and don't clutter the room. Whether you select renovated antiques or fashionable new designs, what's important is that the scheme makes a big impression with the least amount of fuss.

🔺 **A fabulous combination of textures: diamond-sawn slate wall tiles, a wood, chrome and glass basin, and thickly ribbed towels.**

◀ **An antique French chair is partly decorative, partly functional in the corner of a bathroom. Its worn metal works well with the roughly painted wall and reclaimed stone flags.**

A roll-top bath with a tall canopy is the focal point in this dramatic bathroom. Soft, sheer and light, the muslin hanging contrasts pleasantly.

bathing beauties

The raw, hard, unfinished textures of natural materials – such as slate, terracotta, plaster, and ceramic – can often be the ideal complement to the bold tones of a simple structural

544 HONED SLATE
The interesting texture of slate is highly suitable for a classic-style bathroom.

ROUGH TERRACOTTA
Old and roughly pitted terracotta has a fabulously earthy, rustic texture.

482 PITTED PLASTER
A bare, distressed plaster wall can make a striking statement.

SPONGED PAINTWORK
Sponging over a wet paint color gives a wall a three-dimensional appearance.

146 WOVEN FABRIC
A bathroom window dressing need not be too grand or complex.

CERAMIC TILES
Vivid tiling – here with contrast grouting – adds color and texture.

swatch

▲ A hard wood floor and a soft wool rug: practical and comfortable in this home office, which has plenty of clever decorating ideas.

Bright and businesslike

SURROUNDING YOURSELF WITH VIVID COLOR WILL BRIGHTEN UP YOUR
WORKING ENVIRONMENT – BOTH LITERALLY AND EMOTIONALLY. LIFT YOUR SPIRITS
WITH BOLD PRIMARY SHADES AND A VARIETY OF FEEL-GOOD TEXTURES.

bright and businesslike

Simple, attractive materials in a range of textures provide the solution for a smart and achievable home work room.

Home office textures

METAL MESH
Take a wastepaper basket made of metal mesh as a counterpoint to other, more solid, surfaces.
455

BAMBOO FLOORBOARDS
Amazingly tough and durable, bamboo makes a good choice for the floor of a home office.
506

LAMINATE SURFACE
Laminates – such as this lively embossed surface – can be used all over an office, from desktops to cupboard doors.
384

ACRYLIC SHEETING
Likewise, acrylics are ever-present in modern office furniture, and come in some glorious, intense colors.
361

CORK TILES
A cork noticeboard is one way to store memos and display mementoes, at the same time as providing another textural contrast.
305

WOOL CARPET
Don't forget home comforts like a toe-curlingly soft rug with deep woolen tufts.
262

Simple and inexpensive furniture that's both good-looking and practical is ideal when you're working from home, and a large desk, capacious storage and professional-quality chair are good places to start.

Here, a combination of white and apple green has been used for a cheerful, informal feel, teamed with touches of yellow, red and blue – it's certainly not your conventional, stuffy office. Note, too, how the textures vary in a pleasantly subtle way: the smooth hardness of the laminate desktop and storage units contrasts with the nubbly chair fabric, the soft pile of the rug, the opaque plastic of the computer casing and the wired-metal wastepaper basket. And, as a base to it all, the wooden floor has a gentle sheen and pretty pale color that reflect the light and make the room more airy and inviting.

Intelligent innovations

There are some clever touches in this room that are worth emulating if you're thinking of setting up a home office of your own. The desk, for example, is curved for ease of working (with an attractive organic look) and has extending legs so you can adjust it to your height. The storage units dispense with unnecessary handles in favor of cut-out, circular finger-pulls, while the notice-board is simply a magnetized metal sheet. Finally, if you need to maximize every inch of your space (as most home offices do) consider wall-mounting your telephone, propping equipment on the tops of medium-height cabinets and buying a stool for your visitors to sit on – it simply tucks under the desk when not in use.

◀ Think through how much storage you'll need in advance, and plan what will go where; it will save time and effort in the long run.

▶ A slender chair with clean lines and a simple shape will help your office feel less cluttered.

Child's play

PLAYROOMS SHOULD BE FUN AND FUNCTIONAL, STIMULATING YET SAFE. CREATE A FABULOUS KID'S ROOM BY USING VIVID COLORS COMBINED WITH HARD-WEARING, EASY-TO-CLEAN MATERIALS.

◀ The structural components of this room are neutral, while the cushions, blinds and toys provide bright splashes of color.

▼ These stackable cubes are an eye-catching method of storage.

▼ Wooden furniture is a tough and good-looking choice for a child's room.

Children's toys almost inevitably come in bright colors, which means you can design a playroom using fairly neutral shades and still end up with a look that has enjoyable impact. Wooden furniture is sturdy, inexpensive and easy to care for; if, however, you (or your children) prefer a more vivid scheme it can always be painted or stained. After tables and chairs, storage is probably the biggest question in designing this type of room: chests or boxes in wood or plastic, preferably on casters for flexibility, are probably the most practical, and can be as plain or as colorful as you wish. For painting, drawing and homework, provide a solid, spacious desk and a chair with good support.

Writing on the wall

On the walls, washable wallpaper in a subtle background color, inexpensive white emulsion (simply wash another coat over if it gets dirty) and blackboard paint are all good solutions. A playroom floor needs to be tough and durable, but at the same time soft on the feet. Wooden boards with comfortable (and sound-muffling) non-slip rugs, a carpet in a color that won't show the dirt, vinyl sheeting or maybe even rubber would all be practical and good-looking.

Beanbags or large floor cushions are ideal for lounging around, and will provide a cozy texture to contrast with wood and plastic. Choose fabrics you can easily unzip and throw into the washing machine, and bold shades that give the whole look an attention-grabbing verve and vitality.

swatch

child's play

The materials you pick for a child's bedroom or playroom need to be hard-wearing, long-lasting, and preferably washable. Within these limits, however, there's plenty of scope for experimenting with textures that will both look and feel great.

Child-friendly textures

BOUCLE WOOL
It's tough and won't show the dirt, but this fabric is also enormously tactile.
128

WALLPAPER
This wallpaper looks just like colorwashed wood, but is much cheaper and easier to instal.
327

TOUGH COTTON
Thick cotton such as this is ideal for a chair or beanbag cover, and has a ribbed surface that makes a pleasant change from smoother canvas.
163

LINOLEUM
A grey lino with a small pattern will hide the dirt; it's inexpensive, soft underfoot, and easy to maintain.
339

▲ Beanbags are perfect for a child's playroom. Use a tactile fabric for the cover, but make sure it's washable.

CHOOSE YOUR MATERIALS WITH CARE.
FROM **PITTED** STONE TO
SHINY GLASS, **SMOOTH**
EMULSION TO **SOFT** SUEDE, EACH
HAS ITS OWN **QUALITIES** AND
USES – PLUS, OF COURSE, A
UNIQUE TEXTURAL EFFECT.

Practical information

PAINT

Walls

Matte paints are generally used for walls and ceilings. Water-based, they cover well, dry easily, and give a smooth, matte surface. For a less standard finish, however, there is a wealth of more specialist paints available, including milk (casein) paints, soft distemper/whitewash, limewash, and various glazes and varnishes. Greater depth can be achieved with the application of special finishes such as dragging, sponging, rag-rolling, or stippling.

Woodwork

The standard finish for woodwork is oil-based eggshell or gloss (although water-based varieties are also available), which are durable and easy to wipe clean. A special paint effect, such as graining, marbling, or tortoiseshelling, adds interest.

Furniture

Flat oil paint is a good choice for painting furniture, protected, if necessary, with layers of clear varnish. Another good choice is eggshell or even matte paint, covered with matte varnish. Distressing, crackleglazing, marbling, and gilding are among the many techniques available, either to disguise inferior wood or simply for decorative fun.

PAPERS

Conventional wallpapers

Wallpaper offers character and is a good way to disguise less than perfect walls. The paper may be smooth or slightly three-dimensional featuring a raised or textured surface, and patterns can vary from small and intricate to modern versions with one, large graphic image per panel. Standard wallpapers will be spongeable (they can be wiped gently with soapy water), washable (they are covered with a thin plastic film and can be cleaned with water) or vinyl (they are covered with a tough plastic coating that means they can be scrubbed, making them a good choice for kitchens and bathrooms). It's a good idea to use inexpensive lining paper if your walls have imperfections that need disguising or prior to hanging heavy or expensive wallpapers; lining paper also provides a good base for painting. Always strip away old wallpaper before hanging new to provide a better base.

Unusual papers

Paper-backed surfaces such as grasscloth, thin cork, wood veneer, silk, woven raffia, metallic foil, and hessian make an interesting

---

swatch

paint effects

A painted surface can provide a neutral background for other features in a room, or – if you use a paint effect – can add subtle interest in its own right. Traditional paint effects include dragging, combing, and rag-rolling, while contemporary effects range from waxing and liming to crackling and splattering.

STIPPLING · STIPPLING · SPONGING · SPONGING · SPATTERING

RAGGING · RAGGING · COLORWASHING · DRYBRUSHING · DRAGGING

DRAGGING · COMBING · CRACKLE · CRACKLEGLAZE · WAXING

LIMING · DISTRESSING · VERDE ANTICO · ANTIQUING · BRASS FINISH

Hand-stripping standard wallpaper

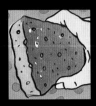

1 Dampen old wallpaper with warm water, and sponge until the old paste is loosened and the paper is soft.

2 Scrape the paper off with a scraper, keeping it flat to wall to avoid gouging holes in plaster. Once the wall is smooth, allow it to dry before applying wallpaper or paint.

Machine-stripping wallpaper

1 Hire a steam stripper from your local tool shop. A stripper generates steam through the plate that is held against the wall, loosening the paper.

2 Scrape off the paper with a hand scraper.

Stripping paper-backed vinyl paper

1 Loosen a corner of paper and pull the top plastic layer back – upward not outward. The backing paper can be left as lining for the next wallcovering.

Stripping waterproof wallpaper

1 Use a sharp implement or serrated scraper to break through the surface.

2 Dampen the wallpaper with warm water. Strip paper as before.

HANGING WALLPAPER

1 Fill cracks and holes with filler. When dry, smooth with an abrasive paper.

2 Measure floor-to-ceiling height and add 3 inches (10 cm) to the total for trimming.

3 Use a plumb bob to ensure your first strip is hanging straight.

4 Measure and cut each piece of wallpaper and lay

right-side down on a clean work-table.

5 Mix the paste according to the packet's instructions. Brush the paste onto the paper, from the center to the edge.

6 Fold paper with pasted area facing inwards and carry it to the wall.

7 Hang the paper, leaving enough overlap at the top for trimming.

8 Brush paper with hanging brush, using long, firm brushstrokes from center of paper to edges.

9 Trim top and bottom of wallpaper.

10 Roll seams with boxwood roller, using sheet of paper to absorb excess paste.

---

statement, and can be hung in much the same way as ordinary wallpapers, either covering a whole wall or as a framed panel. Many types, however, are delicate and difficult to clean, and are thus better suited to low-traffic areas.

Floors

Flooring made from twisted paper yarn, sometimes mixed with sisal, is not nearly as fragile as you might imagine. In fact, it is surprisingly durable, and can be treated in the same way as natural-fiber floorings.

TEXTILES

Drapes

Natural fibers – cotton, wool, silk, and linen – are environmentally friendly, durable, tactile, and hang well. Inexpensive, simple, and versatile, cotton comes in many different weights, from denim to muslin, and finishes, from velvet to chintz. Wool, from soft

cashmere to tough tweed, is flame-retardant and insulating. Silk, usually considered a luxury fabric, also comes in a wide range of weights and finishes; its soft, lustrous fibers make it a good insulator but less durable. Linen can range from crisp and sophisticated to crumpled and soft. It is extremely long-lasting and its matte surface means that it absorbs light.

Natural fibers need to be cleaned carefully or else they may shrink or pucker. Synthetic fibers (the most common are acetate, polyester, acrylic, and viscose) are water- and

STAIN REMOVAL

Always mop up or scrape off spills as soon as possible.

Removing greasy stains
1 Sprinkle an absorbent powder, such as talc, on the spill.
2 After half an hour, vacuum, shake, or brush, then dry clean.

Colorfast linen
1 Stretch the fabric over a basin, sprinkle on powder detergent or stain remover.
2 Pour hot water through the fabric. Rinse. Rub stubborn stains with cleaner, rinse and wash.

Non-washable fabrics
1 Stretch the fabric over a basin, and pour cold water through the stain.
2 Work cleaning solution into stubborn stains, with an absorbent pad placed under the affected area.
3 Sponge with clear water and blot dry.

Emergency upholstery cleaner
1 Mix 1 part detergent to 4 parts boiling water. Cool to a jelly.
2 Whip with egg beater. Use the foam to clean upholstery.

STAIN	METHOD OF REMOVAL
Adhesives (clear and contact, latex, and model-maker's cement)	Apply acetone or non-oily nail varnish remover (except on acetates).
Adhesives (epoxy resin)	Do not allow the adhesive to dry. Apply methylated spirit to natural fabrics and lighter fuel to synthetics.
Adhesives (latex)	Remove with cold water before it dries. Peel off and dab remaining stain with grease solvent.
Adhesives (P.V.A. or craft glue)	Apply methylated spirit.
Beer	Soak fresh stains with detergent or shampoo. For dried stains, use 1 egg cup of white vinegar to 1 pint (600 ml) of water. Blot from non-washables, dab with white vinegar and blot again.
Blood	Soak fresh stains in cold water. Soak up blood from non-washables with an absorbent pad, sponge with cold water containing drops of ammonia. Sponge a dried stain with salt water (1/2 tsp salt to 600 ml/1pint water) or use biological detergent or carpet shampoo.
Candle wax	Chill with an ice cube, then scrape off with a blunt blade. Place slightly damp blotting or tissue paper over and under the wax. Press quickly with a warm iron until the wax is absorbed by the paper.
Chewing gum	Chill with an ice cube, scrape off, then use a dry cleaner.
Coffee/tea/chocolate	If dry, loosen the stain with glycerine. Use carpet shampoo or borax solution (mix one tbsp of borax in 1 pint/600 ml warm water).
Fruit juice	Apply borax solution or carpet shampoo. Sponge with a grease solvent on the wrong side of the fabric.
Ink (ballpoint)	Rinse in cold water, then wash. Dab non-washables with nail varnish remover (except on acetates).
Ink (felt-tip)	Apply methylated spirit.
Lemon juice	Apply borax solution, then wash.
Mildew	Brush off excess, then use carpet shampoo.
Milk	Rinse fresh stains in lukewarm water. Use borax solution or carpet shampoo on dried stains.
Paint (oil and enamel)	Apply paint remover or turpentine.
Paint (fresh latex)	Rinse with cold water.
Soft drinks	Rinse with boiling water, then wash.
Urine	Add 1 egg cup of white vinegar to 1 pint/600 ml of water, or use a biological detergent or shampoo solution.
Wine (white)	Rinse with warm water. If necessary, sponge with borax solution.
Wine (red)	If washable, sponge with white wine, then rinse with warm water. If necessary, sponge with borax solution. Or cover with salt to absorb the wine then stretch the material over a basin and pour through boiling water. If non-washable, use upholstery shampoo or sponge with warm water blot. Sprinkle on talc, leave for one hour. Sponge and blot again.

stain-resistant, strong, and long-lasting; often the most satisfactory fabrics for drapes are made from a blend of man-made and natural fibers. Vacuum drapes gently every month and clean thoroughly every few years; some types can be washed (always follow the manufacturer's advice carefully), others must be dry cleaned. Linings may need to be removed to avoid shrinking at different rates.

Upholstery

Use upholstery-weight fabric that has been rub-tested by the manufacturer. It should also be flame-retardant and, ideally, have been given a stain-resistant treatment. Loose-weave or textured fabrics will snag more easily than smooth, tightly woven fabrics.

SKINS AND FAKE FUR

Leather

Upholstery should be dusted regularly, and occasionally given hide food to prevent it from drying out and to prevent stains. Keep away from direct heat, which may cause cracking. Clean by wiping with a soft, damp cloth. However, some leathers should not be wetted – check the manufacturer's instructions. Leather floors are available in irregularly shaped sheets and tiles. Warm, soft, and quiet underfoot, they need to be waxed regularly and are then relatively easy to keep clean, although they do stain and scratch easily. If treated well, they can last a lifetime, aging naturally like a favorite pair of shoes.

Suede

Suede can be protected with a spray (test first on a hidden area). Wipe dirty suede with a clean, damp cloth and allow to dry naturally. Brush with a suede block. For serious soiling have it professionally cleaned. Alcantara is a cheaper, suede-effect, man-made fabric that can be used in the same way. Nubuck, made from cow leather, looks similar to suede; do not, however, use suede shampoos or brushes on it as they may damage the pile. Use a specialist nubuck or calf-leather cleaner instead.

Fake fur

Fake fur is as attractive and tactile as real fur. It should always be dry cleaned. Clean light soiling by sponging with a warm solution of non-biological washing powder and shaking well before allowing to dry naturally.

CARPET

Carpet is warm and soft underfoot and has good soundproofing and insulating qualities. Its durability and resistance to wear is determined by pile height and density. In general, halls and stairs need heavy-duty carpets, living and dining rooms medium-duty, and bedrooms can be lightweight. Carpets are not usually recommended for bathrooms, kitchens, utility rooms, or conservatories, although some versions are water-resistant.

There are two basic types of carpet construction: woven (very hard-wearing and more expensive) and tufted. Pile types include loop, twist, velvet, cord, shag, saxony, and cut and loop – each gives a different effect and some are more suitable for certain areas than others: shag pile, for example, is dangerous on stairs.

Carpets can be made from a variety of

materials. Of the natural fibers, wool is hard-wearing, relatively easy to clean and fire-retardant; linen, cotton, and silk are wonderfully luxurious, but more decorative than durable. Man-made fibers are less expensive and are often blended with wool to combine their best qualities. A mix of 80 percent wool and 20 percent nylon, for example, is often cited as desirable.

To make your carpet last longer, buy one that has received a stain-resistant/retardant treatment during manufacture and use a high-quality underlay (unless the carpet has its own foam backing). Never use old underlay with a new carpet. Place caster cups under the feet of heavy furniture to minimize denting. Vacuuming a carpet regularly keeps the pile vertical and thus reduces shading, and prevents grit becoming embedded and wearing the fibers away. Mop up spills quickly, rubbing gently from the edge inward. An occasional dry or wet shampoo is usually a good idea – check the care instructions supplied with the carpet. Brand-name stain removers are available; professional cleaning is, however, advisable for stubborn stains.

NATURAL FIBER FLOORINGS

Woven or plaited sisal, coir, seagrass, rush, and jute have been used as floorings for centuries; today they are available in a wide range of colors and patterns, are warm, soundproof, and insulating, and frequently offer good value for money. Coir and sisal, especially, are extremely tough and hard-wearing, though some may find their

rough surface uncomfortable underfoot. For the softest feel in a fiber flooring, opt for jute (though it's the least hard-wearing). Like carpet, natural floorings are not always practical in kitchens or bathrooms, and you should be careful using them on stairs. Rush and jute are not really suitable, while seagrass must be laid with the warp parallel with the stair tread to ensure a good grip. Always consult your retailer for advice on the suitability of a particular fiber flooring for its intended use.

Natural fiber flooring doesn't show dirt badly, but it does need to be vacuumed regularly with a suction (not brush) cleaner. If the covering is not latex-backed, lift it and vacuum the floor underneath, too. Backing and underlay is advisable for fitted floorings, however, for comfort, wear and insulation. And it's a good idea to buy floorings that have already been treated with a stain inhibitor, as stains can be hard to remove. To clean dirt or mud, allow to dry then loosen with a stiff brush before vacuuming. Spills should be blotted promptly with absorbent

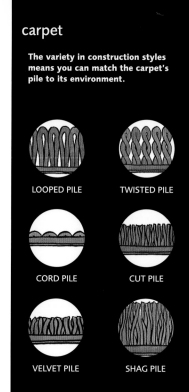

carpet

The variety in construction styles means you can match the carpet's pile to its environment.

LOOPED PILE   TWISTED PILE

CORD PILE   CUT PILE

VELVET PILE   SHAG PILE

sample

paper or a sponge and wiped over with a damp cloth. Dry-cleaning shampoo may get rid of stains. Don't soak sisal, coir, or jute with water or use wet shampoo. Rush, on the other hand, will crumble if it becomes too dry, so it occasionally needs a light spraying of water.

BRICK

Floors

Flooring made of high-fired paving bricks (pavers) is most suitable for hallways, rustic kitchens, dining areas, and conservatories, being non-slip, tough, and rugged in appearance. New or reclaimed bricks come in soft, varied colors and can be laid in a variety of patterns. Though hard and slightly rough underfoot, they're warmer than marble or ceramic tiles. Like any hard surface, however, they will not be kind to dropped crockery. Stains can be hard to remove from brickwork; to avoid staining, bricks may be sealed with boiled linseed oil or polyurethane varnish thinned with white spirit, but it will alter their surface character. Generally, clean by sweeping or use a stiff brush and plain tap water. Always ask your supplier for advice on maintenance.

Interior walls

Indoor walls made of good-condition brick can be left bare, giving an attractively rustic look. To prevent them from shedding fine particles of sand, and to make them easier to clean, seal the walls with P.V.A. adhesive thinned 1:5 with water (this will enrich the color slightly). Alternatively, apply paint straight onto the walls.

CANE

Furniture

Though light and strong, bamboo and rattan furniture can split quite easily, and is then almost impossible to mend – but it will last a long time if well cared for. Clean by wiping with water or a solution of washing-up liquid, but do not over-wet. Do not leave outdoors. If cane furniture does become soaked, allow to dry naturally, away from direct heat.

Floors

Floorboards made from lacquered bamboo are tough, durable, and extremely environmentally friendly. They can be treated like a hardwood floor, with the difference that they're also suitable for use in humid rooms such as bathrooms or conservatories.

CERAMIC TILES

Walls

Ceramic wall tiles are hard-wearing, low-maintenance, and hygienic, and thus highly suitable for hallways, and splashbacks in kitchens and bathrooms. You can lay new tiles directly over old ones, providing the surface is even, or else paint over them. First, wash thoroughly with sugar soap or a detergent solution, then coat with primer followed by a solvent-based paint. To clean, wipe with an all-purpose, anti-bacterial cleaner, avoiding abrasives.

Floors

Thicker than wall tiles, ceramic floor tiles are heat- and water-resistant, hard-wearing and low-maintenance, but may be noisy and tiring on the feet, and are liable to crack if something hard is dropped on them. Use with underfloor heating for warmth. Ideal for bathrooms, kitchens, halls, and conservatories (use frostproof tiles in the latter). Glazed ceramic tiles are slippery when wet: use unglazed (quarry or terracotta), textured, or matte tiles for grip. Terracotta tiles can be sealed with a recommended sealant or with linseed oil and floor wax, which darkens their color slightly. Don't seal or polish non-porous ceramic tiles – the product won't be absorbed, and the tiles will become slippery and attract dirt. Clean ceramic tiles by sweeping, then mopping with a mild detergent. Buff with a soft cloth but don't polish. Harsh abrasives can damage glazed tiles.

Worktops

Tiled kitchen worktops must be laid evenly and flat, and cleaned carefully, as the grout can harbor germs. The tiles are liable to craze and crack if not treated with some care,

ceramic

CLEANING CERAMIC TILES

1 Sweep tiles, then mop with mild detergent, not harsh abrasives.

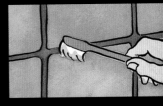

2 Clean dirty grout with an old toothbrush dipped in 1 part bleach to 4 parts water. Then rinse.

3 Buff tiles with a soft cloth – don't polish.

step by step

though individual tiles can be replaced. If grout becomes dirty, use an old toothbrush dipped in one part bleach to four parts water, scrub carefully, then rinse.

CONCRETE

Worktops

Durable and long-lasting, worktops made from reinforced concrete can be custom-molded and colored, with a matte or smooth finish. Seal before use with several applications of an alcohol-based sealant, and finish with wax – this needs to be reapplied occasionally. Clean with a mild, non-abrasive cleaner, such as soap and water.

Floors

Poured concrete floors can be affordable and surprisingly versatile – and are not necessarily for use just in kitchens and conservatories. Though cold and hard underfoot, they are extremely durable and

heat- and scratch-resistant. Left bare, they have a raw, ascetic quality. Less austere finishes include hammering, scoring, sandblasting, painting, staining, veining, polishing (with several coats of wax followed by machine buffing), and imprinting with patterns. Concrete paving can be used exactly like stone slabs. Seal before use to avoid staining – ask your supplier to recommend a suitable sealant.

GLASS

Windows and doors

Alternatives to clear glass include sand-blasted, acid-etched, stained, textured, and patterned – not to mention hi-tech types such as the version that turns from clear to opaque when touched. French windows and large, low panes should be made of toughened or laminated glass, or covered with a special safety film: if broken, they won't shatter into hundreds of dangerously sharp pieces.

As an alternative to chemical window cleaners, use a mix of 2 tbsp or 30ml of vinegar or methylated spirits mixed with 9 pints or 4 liters of water. Apply mixture with a lint-free cloth, and buff the window with scrunched-up newspaper.

Splashbacks

Waterproof, heat-resistant (except under extreme temperatures), and easy to clean, a thick sheet of laminated glass makes a beautiful splashback, though it will scratch or break if struck by a hard object. Lights fitted behind or above make an even bigger impact.

Floors

A glass sheet or block floor (or staircase) makes an impressive statement, though it must be installed by a specialist. It can be very slippery, however, and requires frequent cleaning; opaque glass is a better choice than clear, as scratches won't be so noticeable.

LAMINATES

Work surfaces

Made from a chipboard base topped by a thin sheet of laminate, these inexpensive and low-maintenance surfaces are usually used in kitchens and bathrooms (and sometimes on walls, too). They come in an enormous variety of colors, textures, and patterns, many of them good imitations of stone, wood, and other natural materials, though the surface does, inevitably, feel different. Edges can be square or rounded (post-formed); the latter is less likely to chip. Cheaper versions are sometimes not especially heat- or knife-resistant – high-pressure laminates are a better choice for long-lasting kitchen worktops. Ensure that the underside is sealed, to prevent water damage from appliances placed underneath. To clean, wipe with an all-purpose, anti-bacterial cleaner. Stains can be removed with a slightly abrasive cream cleaner, diluted bleach or even a solvent such as methylated spirits, white spirit, or nail varnish remover (check with the manufacturer first). Chips in laminated surfaces can usually be filled with a purpose-made laminate repairer applied in several thin layers.

step by step

glass

CLEANING WINDOWS

1 Use a lint-free cloth to apply a mix of 2 tbsp (30ml) vinegar or meths with 9 pints (4 liters) of water.

2 Buff with scrunched-up newspaper.

step by step

metal

REPAINTING PAINTED METAL AND WROUGHT-IRON FURNITURE

1 Annually, remove rust with wire wool.

2 Apply anti-rust primer immediately.

3 Apply a coat of exterior metal paint.

4 If furniture is cast-aluminum, wipe with a solution of detergent and paint over any chips with metal paint.

Man-made solid surfaces

Made with a combination of minerals and acrylic resin, these composite surfaces are non-porous, stain-resistant, easy to clean, and come in a wide range of colors and patterns. They can be manufactured to any seamless shape, but they must be professionally installed. They are heat- and stain-resistant, and it is possible for slight burns or scratches to be sanded out (severe damage should be repaired by the manufacturer). Wipe with an all-purpose, anti-bacterial cleaner. Abrasive cream cleaners can be used on stained surfaces, as can solvents, though the latter should always be thoroughly rinsed away.

METAL

In the kitchen

Sheet-metal work surfaces, sinks, and splashbacks are hygienic, heat-proof, and very durable, but tend to scratch, show fingermarks, and eventually assume a natural, worn-in patina. Brushed stainless steel is expensive but usually regarded as the most desirable; galvanized steel looks more industrial but is cheaper. Clean frequently with a non-abrasive liquid or cream; stainless steel can be treated occasionally with baby oil for protection. Bleaching may cause corrosion. Zinc and anodized aluminum are best used for splashbacks only; the former marks easily and dulls over time, resulting in a characterful appearance, while the latter is non-corrosive and light, but dents rather easily and will eventually become soft and dull in appearance.

Garden furniture

Repaint cast- and wrought-iron chairs and tables annually – after first rubbing down with wire wool – using anti-rust primer and exterior metal paint. Cast-aluminum furniture doesn't rust; simply wipe with a solution of washing-up liquid, and touch up chips with metal paint.

Floors

Sheet- or tiled-metal floors (made of stainless or galvanized steel, aluminum, copper, or zinc) are highly tough and resilient, though they do eventually wear to a pleasant patina. Finishes vary from brushed or polished, to oxidized or pressed with a diamond pattern for better grip. Sheets of metal should be welded to a level timber base in order to minimize tinny noise. Ask your supplier for advice on sealing and cleaning.

Door knobs

Door furniture (knobs, handles, and fingerplates) is usually lacquered by the manufacturer, and so simply needs dusting and occasional washing in a soapy solution. Avoid abrasive cleaners that can damage the surface.

PLASTER

Plaster walls and ceilings are traditionally covered with wallpaper, paint, tiles, or some other form of surface. But don't rule out bare plaster, which can be surprisingly attractive, as well as relatively durable and inexpensive. You could choose the more usual finishes such as the standard buff pink, white (with the addition of kaolin), textured (with the application of, perhaps, straw, sand, or sawdust), combed into patterns, sparkled (by working in marble or metallic dust), polished, or stained. Plaster doesn't take kindly to water, however. Make sure that you instal a splashback to protect bare plaster walls in the kitchen or bathroom. Unusual plaster and plaster-like finishes, such as stucco, gesso, fresco, scagliola, and marmorino, also create impressive effects.

SHEET FLOORINGS

Though not especially luxurious, these floorings are quiet, soft, and warm underfoot, strong, flexible, low-maintenance, and easy to clean. They're relatively inexpensive and easy to install, and computer-controlled cutting allows an extensive variety of patterns. These floorings are also available as tiles.

Vinyl

A P.V.C.-based, man-made material, vinyl comes in a variety of textures, patterns, colors, and thicknesses. Thin vinyls can be cold and hard; thicker vinyl is more expensive but also more cushioning, durable, and insulating. Some types are excellent imitations of wood or stone flooring. Vinyl is waterproof and stain-resistant, but may burn, scratch, and dent. If constantly soaked, it may lift up, and less expensive vinyls may discolor with age. Vacuum or sweep regularly to keep clear of grit, which will damage its surface. Wash with a mild washing-up liquid solution or a recommended cleaner, and rinse thoroughly. Avoid harsh abrasives and polishes; the former may mar the surface, the latter may make it slippery. The manufacturer's recommended floor dressing should help reduce staining.

Linoleum

Linoleum – or lino – is made from linseed oil, ground cork, wood flour, and resins, pressed onto a jute or hessian backing. It's resistant to stains, abrasions, and burns, as well as being non-slip, and available in a huge range of colors and patterns. For extra cushioning or sound insulation, or where the sub-floor is particularly uneven, you can buy lino that is backed with cork. Clean regularly by sweeping and washing with a mild detergent solution and, if you wish, applying a water-based emulsion polish. Don't wax polish lino, though, and avoid strong alkaline cleaning agents. Instead, revive worn lino with a special linoleum paint. And avoid allowing water to get underneath it, too, as this will cause it to lift.

Cork

Environmentally friendly cork is lightweight yet hard-wearing, cushioning, and excellent for insulation, though it will lift if laid on a damp floor or over underfloor heating. Cork floors should usually be sealed with a polyurethane varnish. They can be sanded down (and resealed) if worn. Mop with a

vinyl

REPLACING VINYL TILES

1 Heat the damaged tile with a hot iron to soften the adhesive. Lift a corner of the old tile with a filling knife and peel off the tile.

2 Remove the old adhesive with a scraper and clean the area. Trim a new tile to fit.

3 Evenly apply vinyl-tile adhesive to the area with an adhesive spreader.

4 Warm a new tile with an iron. Once placed, lay a board over the tile and weigh it down until the adhesive sets.

washing-up liquid solution and, if you wish, emulsion-polish occasionally to give added protection.

Rubber

Flexible, waterproof, and tough, rubber can be colored, patterned, smooth, or studded and is often considered a good option for a bathroom or hallway (smooth versions, however, may be slippery when wet – consult your retailer for advice). Rubber can be left matte or polished; the latter intensifies color and makes it less liable to mark and stain. Dirt tends to gather on textured surfaces, and watch out for hot items, which may burn the rubber. Sweep and mop clean with a mild detergent. A natural bristle brush (or even an old toothbrush!) can loosen dirt in pattern treads.

STONE

Stone is unbeatably elegant, comes in a variety of subtle natural tones and will last a lifetime (or more) with little maintenance. However, it is also expensive and generally considered cold, noisy, and hard on the feet.

Floors

There are three categories of stone. The "softest" are sandstone and limestone, which can be given a honed (smooth and matte) or sanded (rougher) finish, and contain obvious flecks, fossils, and sediment formations. Because they're porous they need to be sealed to prevent staining; the best method is by silicone impregnation, which hardly changes the surface and allows the stone to age naturally. Sweep and wash regularly with a mild soap.

Slate is a harder stone, almost as durable as marble and granite, and can be finished in various textures: riven (unevenly hand-split), flame-textured (machine-cut with the surface roughened by a flame), sanded (flat but not polished), honed (smooth and matte), and polished. To prevent oil stains, slate may be sealed with a recommended sealer. It can be cleaned by buffing with a nylon pad; neutral detergent may get rid of stains.

Marble, which can be highly polished or left matte, is extremely dense and can be precision-cut; it's impervious to water and is, therefore, a good choice for bathrooms, though it can be slippery when wet. It's best avoided in a kitchen, however, as it can be stained and corroded by acidic solutions. It requires hardly any cleaning other than a rub with a chamois leather dipped in clean water.

Granite is the most durable of all building stones. It's very suitable for kitchens, though polished versions are highly slippery when wet, so it may be better to choose a honed or etched version. Clean with water and never apply floor polish, as this will attract dirt.

Finally, terrazzo is an equally durable but less expensive marble/granite substitute, made of a mix of marble chippings in a cement base, formed into tiles or laid wet directly onto the floor.

Worktops

Polished or honed granite, slate, and terrazzo work surfaces look attractive and are heat-proof, hard-wearing, and impervious to water (slate must be sealed to reduce porosity), but are expensive and tricky to install. Use limestone and marble with caution: both can scratch and stain easily; they must be treated with a solvent-based stone sealant. Clean stone worktops by wiping with a mild anti-bacterial cleaner and drying thoroughly with a soft cloth. Avoid acidic or abrasive cleaners.

WOOD

Floors

Although not as cozy underfoot as carpet, wooden floors are good-looking, available in a variety of styles, and don't harbor dust. Because they can sometimes warp, they are not suitable for conservatories or very wet or steamy bathrooms.

Solid wood floors are usually made of a hardwood such as oak, beech, ash, maple, or mahogany, and come in boards or blocks in a range of thicknesses (the thicker the wood, the longer it will last but the more it will cost). When buying new hardwood, ensure that it comes from an environmentally friendly source. Alternatively, recycled wood can be extremely attractive. Softwoods, such as pine or spruce, wear more quickly; hardwood floors, however, can last a lifetime.

Less expensive is a multi-layered or veneered wood floor, where a thin hardwood surface covers a base of cheaper wood, M.D.F., cork, or plywood. These can be more sound-absorbent than solid wood floors, but won't last as long.

Wood floors should nearly always be sealed. Waxed floors need regular polishing and re-waxing – and beware slippery rugs (special underlay reduces this problem). Oiled wood floors have a mellow sheen; similarly, they need regular re-oiling. Varnish or lacquer, in matte or gloss, is highly durable, especially if painted on in many thin layers, and sanded between each application. Floor paints or stains can be used to disguise inferior wood.

Wooden floors can be damaged by cigarettes, high heels, and furniture; to avoid the latter, place protective pads under furniture. Damage to a solid wood floor can, however, be sanded out. Clean wooden floors by regular sweeping or vacuuming, and wiping with a damp mop. Spills should be mopped up immediately.

Kitchen worktops

Solid wood work surfaces are relatively heat-resistant, and minor burns or knife marks can simply be sanded out. They do, however, need to be well-sealed for both hygiene and durability. A coating of varnish, linseed oil, or beeswax will do the trick; all need regular top-ups. When cleaning, avoid harsh detergents, and dry thoroughly afterward.

Furniture

Lacquered-wood furniture doesn't need polishing; just wipe it with a damp duster. Grease can be removed with a mild solution of soap flakes. For unsealed (waxed or French polished) wooden furniture, simply dust with a dry cloth and apply a wax polish once or twice a year. Remove sticky marks in the same way as above, drying the wood carefully with a soft cloth afterward.

---

step by step

wood

SANDING FLOORBOARDS

Hire an industrial sanding machine from your local tool outlet for main floor area and a smaller hand disc sander for edges. Clear the room of furniture, curtains, and pictures. Close and seal doors with masking tape. Open windows. Remember to wear face mask.

1 Before switching on a sanding machine, tilt it back to lift it off the floor. Switch on and slowly lower onto floor.

2 Sand parallel to the floorboards, never across. Move the machine forward and backward, but keep it moving to avoid making a groove in the floorboards.

3 Sand the edges of the room with a smaller rotary sander. Again, tilt the sander back before switching on and lower gently onto floor.

4 Finish the areas closest to the wall and corners with a scraper. Vacuum the floor and wipe with a cloth dampened with white spirit.

Index

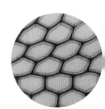